People
of the
West

Based on the Public Television Series

THE WEST

People
of the
West

by Dayton Duncan

With an Introduction by
Stephen Ives and Ken Burns

Little, Brown and Company

Boston   New York   Toronto   London

For Will, my adventurous son and future explorer of the West

•◆• •◆• •◆•

First Edition

Photography credits appear on page 120.

Quotations by Teddy Blue Abbott from *We Pointed Them North: Recollections of a Cowpuncher,*
by E. C. Abbot and Helena Huntington Smith. Norman, Okla.: University of Oklahoma Press, 1939.

Quotations by Buffalo Bird Woman and Wolf Chief from *The Way to Independence: Memories of a Hidatsa Indian Family,*
1840–1920, by Carolyn Gilman and Mary Jane Schneider. St. Paul: Minnesota Historical Society Press, 1987.

Library of Congress Cataloging-in-Publication Data
Duncan, Dayton.
    People of the West / by Dayton Duncan ; with an introduction by
Stephen Ives and Ken Burns. — 1st ed.
        p.   cm. — (The West (Television program))
    Based on the public television series The West.
    Includes bibliographical references and index.
    Summary: Tells the stories of fifteen men and women whose
individual experiences provide a representative picture of life
during the formative years of the American West.
    ISBN 0-316-19627-4 (hc)
    ISBN 0-316-19633-9 (pb)
        1. West (U.S.) — History — Juvenile literature.   2. West (U.S.) —
Biography — Juvenile literature.   [1. West (U.S.) — Biography.
2. Frontier and pioneer life.]   I. Title.   II. Series.
    F591.D84   1996
    978 — dc20   95-41641

10 9 8 7 6 5 4 3 2

Q-KP

Published simultaneously in Canada by Little, Brown & Company (Canada) Limited
and in Great Britain by Little, Brown and Company (UK) Limited

Printed in the United States of America

Contents

Introduction

The story of the West is one of the most important and dramatic stories of our nation's history. In part, it is the story of a landscape unlike any other on earth—vast, treeless prairies, scorching deserts, and majestic mountains, all lying between the Mississippi River and the Pacific Ocean.

But at its heart, the story of the West is about people, about how they responded to that land and how they responded to each other. It is about the many different hopes, dreams, and visions that people in the West pursued—sometimes successfully, sometimes tragically.

Like the landscape itself, the people of the West have always been diverse. No collection of fifteen lives could ever fully illustrate all of the different

experiences of such a rich and varied multitude. But in choosing these individuals from our documentary film series *The West*, we selected people whose lives represent distinctly different aspects of that larger experience.

Most of the people in this book are not well known, although their lives were no less remarkable than those of more famous westerners. Within their stories can be found as much adventure, discovery, personal courage, unrelenting hardship, and undying hope as in any biographies—or Hollywood movies—about more familiar figures. These people have been chosen not for their celebrity, but for the way their *individual* experiences demonstrate what many typical people went through as they tried to make the West their home.

And in following each one, you will not only meet a compelling person from the past but will also witness some of the important milestones of Western history. From the first encounters between Native Americans and Europeans, to the later struggles over Indian lands and Indian culture; from mountain men, missionaries, and Mormons, to prospectors, cowboys, and homesteaders; from those who arrived from every corner of the globe seeking wealth, freedom, or a new chance, to those who found

themselves and their dreams displaced by the newcomers—in following their *collective* experience, a larger history emerges.

It, too, is not complete. The West's history is also like its landscape—too vast to cover quickly or entirely. But taken together, these stories cover more ground than they might appear to at first. History is the collection of stories people tell about the past to explain the present, and the most memorable stories usually center on the actions and dreams of remarkable human beings. *People of the West* tells the stories of fifteen such memorable people. When you look up after following them all, you may be surprised to see how far the journey has taken you.

—Stephen Ives and Ken Burns

Sweet Medicine

Centuries ago, when the West belonged to Native Americans alone, a boy named Sweet Medicine was born to the Cheyenne tribe. Cheyenne tradition says that as a young man Sweet Medicine traveled on his own to the Black Hills. There, the storytellers say, he spent several years underneath a big mountain with the *maiyun*—"the mysterious ones," godlike beings whose extraordinary powers could control the events of humans and nature. They taught Sweet Medicine many things and gave him great spiritual powers of his own so that he could help his people when he returned.

It was said that when the Cheyenne were hungry, Sweet Medicine sang a special song for four nights that summoned a buffalo herd to their camp and kept them from starvation. And at times, the stories say, he changed himself into different animals—a coyote, a fox, a magpie, even an owl.

But the reason the Cheyenne still honor Sweet Medicine in their stories is because of the important values he preached—and because, they say, he predicted the future that lay ahead for the Cheyenne and all other Native peoples of the West.

•◆• •◆• •◆•

"The mysterious ones" had given Sweet Medicine four sacred arrows to protect the Cheyenne. In order for the arrows' powers to work, the Cheyenne would have to perform special ceremonies and obey laws that the maiyun had taught him. Two of the arrows were for use in war against their enemies, and two were to bring success in hunting.

Sweet Medicine set up a council of forty-four chiefs to be in charge of making decisions for the tribe. He told them that while the chiefs should be brave in battle, it was even more important that they be generous and wise. "You chiefs are peacemakers," he told them. "Though your son

Cheyenne peace chiefs

might be killed in front of your tepee, you should take a peace pipe and smoke. Then you would be called an honest chief."

In addition to the council of chiefs, he organized four warrior societies—the Swift Foxes, the Elks, the Red Shields, and the Bowstrings—each with its own ceremonies and costumes. Their duties included enforcing tribal laws, supervising the movement of camps, and fighting bravely. Young men in one society, the Swift Foxes, carried a rope and lance into battle. To prove their valor, they sometimes drove the lance into the ground and tied themselves to it, vowing to stand there until either they were killed or the enemy retreated.

Sweet Medicine advised the Cheyenne to be clean and healthy, to take pride in themselves, to avoid arguing with one another, and especially never to kill members of their own tribe. The punishment for murder, he said, would be exile. And a special ceremony would have to be held, purifying and renewing the sacred arrows so that one person's crime would not bring bad fortune on everyone else. During the sacred renewal ritual, carried on by the chiefs, no noise was allowed in camp, personal disputes were prohibited, and all Cheyenne were required to be friendly toward each other. Members of the warrior societies were posted throughout the village to make sure the rules were followed.

For many years Sweet Medicine stayed with his people. But then he grew old and realized he was about to die. He told the warrior societies to build a tepee of cedar poles with a grass bed inside and to carry him to it. There, in his final days, he spoke to them about the future.

"Listen to me carefully," he said. "There are all kinds of people on earth that you will meet someday." Some

You chiefs are peacemakers. Though your son might be killed in front of your tepee, you should take a peace pipe and smoke. Then you would be called an honest chief.

— Sweet Medicine

Cheyenne warrior

Before horses were brought to North America, dogs carried Indians' belongings.

would have black skins, he predicted, but most would be white, with beards on their faces and strange clothing on their bodies.

"These people do not follow the way of our great-grandfather," he warned. "They follow another way. They will be people who do not get tired, but who will keep pushing forward, going, going all the time. They will be looking for a certain stone. They will travel everywhere, looking for this stone which our great-grandfather put on the earth in many places."

When Sweet Medicine lived, there were no horses in North America. Indians in the West had to hunt buffalo by foot, and they used dogs to carry their few belongings when they moved their villages. The strangers, he said, would bring with them an animal with a shaggy neck and tail almost touching the ground. "This animal will carry you on its back and help you in many ways," Sweet Medicine predicted. "Those far hills that seem only a blue vision in the distance take many days to reach now. But with this animal, you can get there in a short time, so fear him not."

There are all kinds of people on earth that you will meet someday. There will be many of these people, so many that you cannot stand against them.... They will try to change you from your way of living to theirs, and they will keep at what they try to do.

— Sweet Medicine

He added, however, that the strangers would bring many other changes that would not be so helpful. They would have "something that makes a noise and sends a little round stone to kill," and with it they eventually would eliminate the buffalo herds so important to the survival of the

As Sweet Medicine prophesied, horses and guns changed Indian lives. Here, a battle scene is drawn on a buffalo hide.

Cheyenne and other tribes. These strangers would eat another animal "with a head like a buffalo, but white horns and a long tail," he said.

As he looked ahead, Sweet Medicine said he also saw strange things, carrying more than one person, going up and down rivers and moving quickly across the dry land of the West.

"There will be many of these people," he said, "so many that you cannot stand against them. They will work with their hands. They will tear up the earth. They will try to change you from your way of living to theirs, and they will keep at what they try to do."

Sweet Medicine begged his people to remember what they had learned from him. "Live the way I have taught you," he said, " and follow the laws. You must not forget them, for they have given you strength." If they *did* forget him and his teachings, he warned, they would become "worse than crazy." Then Sweet Medicine died.

In the stories the Cheyenne tell about their prophet Sweet Medicine, they point out that most of his predictions came true.

The strangers he foresaw did arrive in the West. Some came searching for gold. Others wanted to plow and farm the land. Still others hoped to

Three Cheyenne women

change the Indians by converting them to new religions and new ways of living. The newcomers brought horses, which the Cheyenne and other tribes gladly mastered, but also cattle, which took over the grasslands after the buffalo were slaughtered by hunters using powerful guns.

The buffalo will disappear, and another animal will take its place, a slick animal with a long tail and split hoofs, whose flesh you will learn to use.

— *Sweet Medicine*

Over the years, the newcomers arrived in increasing numbers, by wagon and boat, and then by a new railroad that stretched all the way to the sea. And as they came, they changed the West—and the lives of the people who had first lived there—forever.

But just as other Native Americans remember their ancestors by telling their stories and honoring their traditions, many Cheyenne still talk with respect about Sweet Medicine and his teachings. And in that way, they spare themselves his last prediction—that they would become "worse than crazy" if they ever forgot his teachings.

Cabeza de Vaca

On November 6, 1528, about eighty Spanish soldiers stumbled onto the shore of what is now Texas. Their boats had just been shipwrecked. They were wet and cold, weak from hunger and sickness. And they were immediately surrounded by two hundred Indians armed with bows and arrows.

Spain already controlled South and Central America, the Caribbean islands, and Mexico. But these Spaniards were the first Europeans ever to set foot in the region that would become the American West. They had planned to come as conquerors. Instead, they arrived as helpless captives.

Eventually only four would survive. Over the next eight years, these four would wander sixteen hundred miles across seemingly endless plains and scorching deserts, seeking to reach their own people in Mexico.

How they managed to live, the wonders that they saw, the hardships they endured, and the Indians they met—all were described in a report written for the king of Spain by one of the survivors, Alvar Núñez Cabeza de Vaca.

Cabeza de Vaca's report was the first eyewitness account of the West by a white man. It is also one of the West's most remarkable stories—and lessons.

•◆• •◆• •◆•

At first the Indians of the Texas coast welcomed the men who had washed up on shore. These strangers, with their hairy faces and white skin, looked different from any people the Indians knew. Most Indian men had less facial hair and used shells to pull out what few whiskers grew on their cheeks. Equally strange was a large man with black skin—a North African slave named Esteván, who had been brought along on the Spanish expedition. The Indians had never seen such people before, and they thought the newcomers might be healers or medicine men, with special powers.

My life had become unbearable.... My fingers got so raw that if a straw touched them, they would bleed.
— *Cabeza de Vaca*

Cabeza de Vaca and the others were given food and shelter by the natives. But when most of the sick and weakened Spaniards died anyway, the Indians decided these white men were not sent by the gods after all, and they put the few survivors to work as slaves.

"My life had become unbearable," Cabeza de Vaca wrote. He had to dig for roots with his bare hands and carry wood on his naked back. "I had to work amidst them without benefit of clothes," he said. "My fingers got so raw that if a straw touched them, they would bleed."

Finally he escaped his masters and went to work as a trader. He began to travel, exchanging goods that one tribe wanted to sell for goods another tribe wanted to obtain. For instance, he traded the coastal tribes' seashells (used for cutting, since the Indians did not have metal) for deerskins and red dirt (used for clothing and face paint) gathered by tribes farther inland.

As he traveled, Cabeza de Vaca learned that the "Indian world" was actually an amazing collection of many worlds. Individual tribes were as different from the others as the nations of Europe—France, Spain, Austria, Denmark, Portugal, Russia, England—were from one another. They, too, had different names: the Hans and the Charrucos, the Miriames and the Quitoks, a tribe Cabeza de Vaca called the People of the Figs, and many, many more. Each spoke a different language. Cabeza de Vaca learned to gesture with his hands, using a common sign language Native Americans had developed to communicate with one another.

And each tribe had different customs. Some hunted barefoot, running down deer. Others set the grasslands on fire to catch rabbits and squirrels. There were tribes that fished and ate oysters, tribes that ate walnuts, and others that loved prickly pear cactus and its juice. Cabeza de Vaca wrote of meeting one tribe so hungry that its people ate "spiders and the eggs of ants, worms, lizards, and the dung of deer."

We traveled in that region through so many different villages of such diverse tongues that my memory gets confused.

— Cabeza de Vaca

Some tribes were fierce and warlike. Others were peaceful. Some seemed always filthy from dirt and dust. Another made a soap from the yucca plant and prided itself on its people's clean skin and smell.

9

Most Indians, he said, "love their offspring the most of any in the world, and treat them with the greatest mildness." But he met one tribe that sometimes killed small boys as a sacrifice to angry spirits that had appeared in dreams. And another one often left baby girls to die in the wilderness, because the tribe had only enough food for a few children and preferred them to be boys, future warriors.

For five years, Cabeza de Vaca roamed as a merchant. "This occupation suited me," he wrote. "I could travel where I wished and was not a slave. Wherever I went, the Indians treated me honorably and gave me food, because they liked my commodities."

But his real goal was to learn enough about the country to help him and the other three survivors from his expedition escape and return to Mexico. In 1534 all four of them—including the black man Esteván—slipped away from their captors and headed west across the vastness of Texas.

No one knows the exact route the four men took. But it was a long, hard trip. And full of surprises.

On the plains they came across an animal that Cabeza de Vaca described as having shaggy hair and small horns. It roamed great dis-

First known drawing of a buffalo published in Europe

tances as it grazed, he said, and the Indians of the area relied on it for food, clothing, and much more. As the first European ever to see these animals, he called them cattle, and said their meat was "finer and fatter than the beef" of Spain. In fact, they were not cows, but buffalo.

Bighorn sheep

The men saw other animals new to Europeans—prairie dogs, armadillos, and bighorn sheep. They swam rivers, passed stony mountains, and crossed the rocky, blistering deserts of West Texas. "Throughout all this country we went naked," Cabeza de Vaca wrote, and their skin constantly peeled away from sunburn. "The country is so broken and thickly set that thorns and shrubs tore our flesh wherever we went."

But they were rarely alone. They met new tribes everywhere they went and further witnessed the great variety of Indian peoples living in the West. One tribe raised beans, pumpkins, and maize (Indian corn); one sometimes ate dogs. One fought wars with poisoned arrows; another greeted strangers by touching their guests' faces and hands, then touching their own bodies.

The Indians treated us kindly. They deprived themselves of food to give to us, and presented us skins and other tokens of gratitude. — Cabeza de Vaca

And they were told of still other tribes who lived farther north, in great cities built into the sides of cliffs, wealthy people with valuable blue gems. It was a story of riches that Cabeza de Vaca knew the king of Spain would want to hear.

Everywhere they went, the three Spaniards and Estevan were welcomed by the tribes, who began to believe that the strangers could heal the sick by blowing air on them, reciting odd-sounding words (a Christian prayer), and making a strange gesture (the sign of the Cross). Hundreds of Indians began to travel with them as they walked through the northern deserts of Mexico.

A Navajo painting of Spanish soldiers on the march

At last, in 1536, Cabeza de Vaca could tell that they were approaching the part of Mexico where Spaniards lived. But it was not as happy a moment as he had hoped.

Spanish soldiers had been in the area, raiding the Indian villages and capturing their people to be sold as slaves to work in mines and on ranches. "The sight was one of infinite pain to us," he wrote, "the hamlets deserted and burned, the people thin and weak, all fleeing or in concealment."

His own experience among Indians over so many years had taught Cabeza de Vaca a different lesson about how Europeans should treat Native Americans to gain their trust and help. "They must be won by kindness," he wrote. That was the only "certain way, and no other is."

Finally twenty Spanish horsemen appeared. They couldn't believe that the four sunburned, half-starved men traveling in friendship with so many Indians were part of the Spanish expedition of conquest that had been lost eight years before.

And the Indians couldn't believe that Cabeza de Vaca and the Spanish soldiers could be from the same group of people. He healed the sick, the Indians said, while the soldiers killed the healthy. He walked barefoot without weapons; the soldiers rode horses and carried lances. He shared, while they robbed. "To the last," he wrote, "I could not convince the Indians that we were of the same people as the Christian slavers."

Many miles and many years earlier, Cabeza de Vaca might have agreed with both the Spanish soldiers—that Indians were worthy only of being slaves—and the Indians—that someone who treated them decently must not be Spanish. But his incredible journey had taught him something new. He could be both a Spaniard *and* a friend to the Indians.

And so, before he and his three companions were taken to Mexico City, Cabeza de Vaca warned his Indian friends to escape while they could. The Spaniards had planned to make them slaves.

Back among his own countrymen, Cabeza de Vaca wrote about his adventure, describing for the first time the people, animals, and lands in the West. And he tried to persuade Europeans that when they dealt with Indians they should "win by kindness" instead of by force.

But many Europeans were far more interested in his reports of cities of great wealth north of Mexico than in his advice for treating with Indians. Even though Cabeza de Vaca had never seen these cities himself, the rumor of their existence would send more Spaniards into the West in the years that followed. Esteván himself would lead one of the first expeditions sent to find the fabled Seven Cities of Gold and would die in a fight with Indians.

Other Europeans came, too—French, English, and Russians. Eventually even representatives of the young nation on the Atlantic Coast, the United States, would make their way west. Over the next three hundred years, their encounters often resulted in conflict, violence, and misunderstanding with Native Americans.

Unfortunately, as more and more outsiders moved into the West, they often forgot the lesson that Cabeza de Vaca, the first white man to visit there, had learned so well.

Kit Carson

Notice is hereby given to all persons,

THAT CHRISTOPHER CARSON, a boy about 16 years old, small of his age, but thick set; light hair, ran away from the subscriber, living in Franklin, Howard county, Missouri, to whom he had been bound to learn the saddler's trade, on or about the first of September last. He is supposed to have made his way towards the upper part of the state. All persons are notified not to harbor, support or assist said boy under the penalty of the law. One cent reward will be given to a by person who will bring back the said boy.

DAVID WORKMAN. 16-3*

Franklin, Oct. 6, 1826

In 1826 a sixteen-year-old boy was working in a saddle maker's shop in Franklin, Missouri. He was small for his age and had never learned to read or write. But all his life he had listened to stories about the adventures of a distant relative, the legendary frontiersman Daniel Boone. Now the boy had become bored with town life and saddle making.

He learned that a wagon train was leaving for Santa Fe, which was then part of Mexico, and slipped away secretly to accompany it. His boss advertised in the local newspapers, asking people to find the boy and return him to his job. As a reward, the saddle maker offered one cent.

But no one ever caught the boy. And he never came back from the West. Instead, Christopher Houston "Kit" Carson became a mountain man — and eventually found as many adventures as his hero Daniel Boone.

14
·◆·

In some ways, a mountain man's job wasn't much more exciting than making saddles. In the southern Rocky Mountains, Carson had to learn how to put a metal trap in a rushing stream with a special bait that attracted beavers. Each evening, he would wade back into the ice-cold water and collect the beavers he had caught. With a knife, he removed the skin and fur from the carcass. Since the beaver's tail was considered a special treat he would save it for his next meal. Back at camp, Carson would stretch and dry the beaver pelt, which would eventually be sent east and used to make the fancy hats that wealthy people in New York, London, and Paris liked to wear.

I discovered some elk on the side of a ridge. I shot one and immediately after the discharge of my gun, I heard a noise to my rear. I turned around and saw two very large grizzly bears making for me. — Kit Carson

It was a hard life. The trappers spent the winters camped in the mountains, waiting for the ice to melt in the beaver streams. In the spring and

Trapping for beaver

fall, they moved constantly, always searching for places that hadn't been overtrapped. Men died of pneumonia from spending so much time in cold water, from snakebites and grizzly bear attacks and gun accidents. Others simply disappeared without a trace. One season, 116 trappers left Santa Fe to trap beaver. A year later, only sixteen of them were still alive.

"Once a year, perhaps, I would enjoy the luxury of a meal consisting of bread, meat, sugar, and coffee," Carson said. The rest of the time, the only food was "that which I could procure with my rifle." When elk, deer, and buffalo could not be found, the men ate their horses or mules. Joe Meek, a friend of Kit Carson's, once ate ants, crickets, and even his moccasins to keep from starving.

Despite their hard work, none of the mountain men became wealthy. A trapper might bring four hundred pelts, worth a thousand dollars or more, to sell at the huge yearly summer encampment called the rendezvous, where furs were traded for supplies and pay. More often than not, however, the trappers would spend all the money they had earned on whiskey, gambling, and tobacco before heading back into the mountains for another year.

Trappers and sailors are similar in regard to the money that they earn so dearly, being daily in danger of losing their lives. But when the voyage has been made and they have received their pay, they think not of the hardships and dangers through which they have passed, but spend all they have and are then ready for another trip.

— *Kit Carson*

But even if the work was grueling and the financial rewards were low, Kit Carson had found what he was looking for when he left Missouri for the Rocky Mountains.

He had found adventure.

At one rendezvous, he challenged a trapper who had been bullying everyone else to a duel.

"We both fired at the same time," Carson said. "I shot him through the arm and his ball passed my head, cutting my hair and the powder burning my eye, the muzzle of his gun being near my head when he fired. During the remainder of our stay in camp, we had no more bother with this bully."

Like all the other mountain men, Carson became good friends with some Indian tribes and a fierce enemy to others. The Blackfeet wounded him in battle, a shot that shattered a shoulder bone. He fought Apaches, Comanches, and Miwoks, and even took scalps from some of the Indians he killed. Because of his small size and his unfailing courage in helping them fight against the Crow, the Cheyenne called him Vih-hiu-nis, "Little Chief."

He married the daughter of an Arapaho chief, but she died after giving birth to their daughter. His second wife, a Cheyenne woman, divorced him according to the traditions of her people, by placing his belongings outside their tepee.

Like Kit Carson, mountain men often married Native American women, as depicted in this painting THE TRAPPER'S BRIDE.

After sixteen years as a trapper, Kit Carson had seen much of the West—the Rocky Mountains, the deserts of the Southwest, the rolling western plains, the central valley of Mexican California—all in a continual search for furs.

But at the end of the 1830s, the fashions in the big cities changed. Rich people began wearing hats made of silk rather than beaver. Carson and the other mountain men suddenly found themselves out of work. Some returned to their homes in the East. Other got jobs leading wagon trains of American pioneers going to Oregon and California.

Kit Carson set out for even more adventures.

He became the scout and guide for Lieutenant John Charles Frémont, sent by the United States government to roam the West and make better maps of it. They went on three important expeditions in the 1840s.

Artist Charles Russell's representation of Kit Carson and his men

With Frémont, Carson explored the Great Salt Lake in Utah on a rubber boat, crossed the blistering deserts of Nevada, and nearly starved to death climbing over the Sierra Nevada, the steep and snowy California mountain range, during winter. On the West Coast, they took part in the war with Mexico that made California part of the United States.

You would not suppose from a glance at the man that he was the hero of so many border exploits — the terror of the wild nomad, the far-famed Kit Carson. I was disappointed at the first sight of the man. —ARKANSAS GAZETTE AND DEMOCRAT, *June 13, 1851*

And on two different occasions, when important news needed to be sent from California to the president, in Washington, D.C., Kit Carson was the man chosen to ride clear across the country to deliver it.

All these exploits—and Frémont's popular reports of them—made Carson famous. Rivers, mountain passes, and towns were named for him. Books began appearing with Carson as their hero. Most of them were written by people who had never been to the West and who had never met Kit Carson. They simply made up their stories about him.

In 1849, the fictional Kit Carson and the real one met for the first time. Word came that the army needed him to help rescue a pioneer woman named Mrs. White, who had been captured by Apaches. He tracked the

One of many books glorifying Carson's "exploits"

Indians for twelve days and finally located their camp. But the army commander ignored Carson's advice to attack immediately, and by the time the troops entered the camp, the Apaches had scattered.

"The body of Mrs. White was found, still perfectly warm," Carson later remembered. "She had been shot through the heart with an arrow not more than five minutes before. She evidently knew that someone was coming to her rescue.

"We found a book in the camp, the first of the kind I had ever seen, in which I was represented as a great hero, slaying Indians by the hundred. I have often thought that Mrs. White must have read it, and knowing that I lived nearby, must have prayed for my appearance in order that she might be saved. I did come, but I lacked the power to persuade those that were in command over me to follow my plan for her rescue. They would not listen to me and they failed."

Kit Carson's later years were as adventurous as his early ones. They were also marked by both success and failure and by being a close friend to some Indian tribes and a hated enemy to others.

During the Civil War, Carson was ordered by General James Carleton to move the twelve thousand Navajos from what is now called the Four

Corners region (where the states of New Mexico, Arizona, Colorado, and Utah meet). Carson could not catch the Navajos in their homeland of canyons and mountains. So he ordered his men to burn the Indians' homes and cornfields, round up their sheep, and cut down their peach trees. Winter came. The Navajos began to freeze and to starve. Old people and young children began dying. Most of the Navajos surrendered.

In what the tribe remembers as the Long Walk, they were forced to march more than three hundred miles to a reservation in eastern New Mexico, where they stayed for four years before being allowed to return to their homeland. During that time, more than two thousand of them died from disease and starvation. To this day, the Navajos have never forgiven Kit Carson for his part in what they call Nahonzod—"the Fearing Time."

But other tribes had a different experience with Carson. As the government agent to the Ute, he worked hard to help the tribe preserve their hunting grounds from settlers and miners. He urged the government to keep the promises it made in its treaties with Indians and to fire agents who cheated the tribes they were supposed to help. Many Indians considered him the bravest and most honest white man they knew and called him Father Kit.

Kit Carson in 1868, shortly before his death

By 1868 Carson was nearly sixty years old and was very sick. He was taken to see a doctor at an army fort in southern Colorado, but his condition grew steadily worse.

He asked that a blanket and a buffalo robe be laid out on the floor of the doctor's office, and his final request, on May 23, was for a buffalo steak and some coffee. And then he died, on the same kind of bed and after eating the same kind of meal he had once dreamed about as a bored teenager working in a saddle maker's shop in Missouri.

Narcissa
Whitman

July 4, 1836—the sixtieth anniversary of the Declaration of Independence—was a historic day for the United States. On that hot summer day, a caravan of horses and wagons reached South Pass, the best path through the Rocky Mountains and the nation's western boundary at the time. For years, such caravans had been arriving from Missouri each summer with supplies for the fur trappers who hunted and lived in the mountains. But there was something new about this caravan—two women from the East were riding along with it.

Narcissa Prentiss Whitman, age twenty-eight, was one of them. From the time she was fifteen, Narcissa had dreamed of leaving New York and traveling west as a missionary to "save" the Indians by converting them to Christianity. Now she was on her way, and at South Pass she became the first white American woman to cross the Continental Divide (where the rivers begin to flow west, toward the Pacific Ocean).

Off in the distance, she saw a cloud of dust and heard the rumble of horses approaching.

"Some ten Indians and four or five white men, whose dress and appearance could scarcely be distinguished from that of the Indians, came in sight over the hills," she wrote. "All gave a yell, such as hunters and Indians can only give; *whiz, whiz,* came their bullets over our heads."

But it was not an attack. It was a "welcoming party" from the mountain man rendezvous, wildly excited and curious to see the eastern women. Most western Indians had never seen a white woman before, and at the rendezvous, Narcissa said, "I was met by a company of native women, one after the other, shaking hands and saluting me with a most hearty kiss."

Although they did not realize it at the time, Narcissa Whitman's journey marked the beginning of a new era in the West. Soon, more and more American families would cross South Pass to settle beyond the Rocky Mountains. The United States would stretch its borders to follow them all the way to the Pacific.

But on that day of celebration in 1836, there was something else no one realized. Tragedy was waiting for Narcissa—and for the Indians she had come west to save.

•◆• •◆• •◆•

Narcissa had grown up in Prattsburg, New York, during a time of great religious revival in the East. Her family devoted their Sundays entirely to worship—two church services, Sunday school, individual and family prayer. The only books allowed in the house dealt with religion, and Narcissa's favorites were about missionaries who brought the story of Jesus to non-Christians, called "heathens."

Narcissa wanted to be a missionary, too, and studied hard to prepare herself. But the Missionary Board would not accept a woman unless she was married. So for ten years Narcissa taught school in New York

An artist's rendering of Marcus Whitman

instead, although she kept sending letters asking for an assignment.

Finally she was contacted by Marcus Whitman, a doctor who had heard of her interest. He was planning to open a mission among the Indians beyond the Rocky Mountains, he said, and he needed a wife to accompany him. Would she be willing? For Narcissa—and Marcus—the commitment to the missionary cause was more important than romantic love. Within two days, they were engaged. And on the day after their marriage in 1836, they left their families and headed west.

"Our desire now is to be useful to these Indians, teaching them the way to salvation," Narcissa wrote. "It is a great responsibility to be pioneers in so great a work. It is with cautious steps that we enter on it."

Narcissa enjoyed the long journey west, even though she and Marcus had to share a small tent with Henry and Eliza Spalding, the other missionary couple in the supply caravan. She learned how to use dried buffalo dung (called buffalo chips) for fuel for their campfires and added, "I never saw anything like buffalo meat to satisfy hunger." At the rendezvous, she and Eliza Spalding handed out Bibles to the rough-looking mountain men, "which might result in the salvation of their souls."

Finally, in late fall, they reached their destination: Oregon Country, which at the time was jointly claimed by both England and the United States. The Spaldings went to settle among the Nez Percé Indians. Narcissa and Marcus Whitman decided to build their mission on the banks of the Walla Walla River, among the Cayuse tribe.

Our desire now is to be useful to these Indians, teaching them the way to salvation.... It is a great responsibility to be pioneers in so great a work. It is with cautious steps that we enter on it.

— *Narcissa Whitman*

Their adventurous journey was over. But the hard part of missionary work was about to begin.

For generations upon generations, the Cayuse had lived in the grassy plains of what is now eastern Washington and Oregon. They moved with the seasons—fishing in the rivers, hunting in the hills, gathering roots in the meadows. To them, the earth was a sacred mother whose children included all of the animals as well as humans, and everything in the world had a spirit.

When they were age ten or eleven, young Cayuse would leave the village to seek a vision and gain a guardian spirit called a *wey-ya-kin*—an animal, rock, even a cloud—that would give them a special song or prayer and with it special powers. A deer *wey-ya-kin,* for instance, might grant swiftness.

The Cayuse had songs, chants, dances, prayers, and special costumes to communicate with spirits before going on a hunt or to war, for marriages and burials, and for help against sickness. They believed that everyone had a soul that lived on in an afterworld, though it was not a heaven or a hell.

All of this seemed strange and forbidding to Narcissa Whitman.

"Never was I more keenly aware of the self-denials of a missionary life," she wrote home. "Even now while I am writing, the drum and the savage yell are sounding in my ears. Dear friends, will you not sometime think of me almost alone in the midst of savage darkness?"

To the Cayuse, much of what the Whitmans preached seemed equally strange. The Indians were willing to learn the Christian rituals (they especially liked the songs), which might connect them to the white man's *wey-ya-kin* and therefore his special powers, such as guns and cattle and metal goods. But the missionaries did not want the Indians simply to add Christian rituals to their lives. They wanted them to abandon their old ways completely. *Wey-ya-kin*s were wrong, the Cayuse were told. Gambling, horse racing, and traditional dancing were to be abandoned. To become farmers

The missionaries' greatest trials are but little known to the churches. I have never ventured to write about them for fear it might do hurt.

— Narcissa Whitman

and plant crops, the Cayuse would have to plow the soil—tearing the flesh of Mother Earth, in their eyes.

And if they didn't do these things, they were told, they were doomed and would go to a terrible place when they died. "Bad talk," the Cayuse called this, and they didn't like it.

A huge gap of misunderstanding and distrust grew between the Whitmans and the Cayuse. The Indians resented Marcus for building his mission and starting his crops on Cayuse land without offering to pay anything for it. Narcissa didn't like having Indians in her house because, she said, "they would make it so dirty and full of fleas that we could not live in it." She began to consider the Cayuse lazy and sullen. They found her snobbish and overbearing.

During eleven years at the mission, the Whitmans converted a Scottish visitor, a French-Canadian, and a few Hawaiian laborers to their faith. But they failed to make a single convert among the Cayuse.

Slowly they shifted their attention to different goals.

•◆•

A sketch of the Whitmans' mission in Oregon

The letters that Narcissa, Marcus, and other missionaries sent back East always mentioned the mild climate and rich soil of Oregon. In 1841 about two dozen American settlers came west in a wagon train to see for themselves. The next year more than a hundred showed up. The years that followed brought thousands.

By 1846 there were only 750 British citizens living in the Pacific Northwest, but there were more

I have no doubt our greatest work is to aid the white settlement of this country and help to found its religious institutions.

— *Marcus Whitman*

than five thousand American settlers. Outnumbered, England dropped its claim on the territory, and Oregon officially became part of the United States.

The Whitman mission had become a welcome resting place for the wagon trains that passed by on the Oregon Trail. "I have no doubt our greatest work is to aid the white settlement of this country," rather than to convert Indians, Marcus admitted.

"My hands and heart are usefully employed," Narcissa wrote home, "not so much for the Indians, as my own family." Her first and only child, Alice Clarissa, had drowned in the Walla Walla River at age two, but Narcissa had begun adopting children, including seven orphans whose parents had died on the trail. She devoted herself to the children—and would not let them mingle with the Indians.

For the Cayuse, the flood of settlers was not so welcome. "The poor Indians are amazed at the overwhelming numbers of Americans coming into the country," Narcissa wrote. "They seem not to know what to make of it."

The pioneers hunted the animals that the Cayuse depended on for food; the wagon trains' oxen ate the grass on which the Indians kept their horses. The Cayuse began to fear that the newcomers were overrunning their land. Tensions grew. Some Indians asked the missionaries to leave— even threatened them—but the Whitmans believed their work was too important to abandon.

Then, in 1847, a wagon train brought measles to Oregon. It was a new disease for the Indians and so hit them the hardest because they had no immunity against it. Despite Marcus's efforts to treat them, half of the Cayuse tribe died, including most of the children.

Noticing that many more Indians than whites had died from the disease, some Cayuse believed that the Whitmans were deliberately trying to kill them all. Perhaps, one said, Marcus was using his special powers to poison them, just as he poisoned the wolves that attacked his livestock.

So much had gone wrong since that day in 1836, when Narcissa had been hugged and kissed by the Indian women at the rendezvous. Despite their eleven years among the Cayuse, she and Marcus never really understood the Indians they had once hoped to "save." And the Cayuse had come to see the Whitmans not as friends but as enemies, symbols of the thousands of other Americans who followed, bringing with them destruction and death.

For their own survival, the Cayuse decided, they must get rid of the missionaries.

On the afternoon of November 29, 1847, two Cayuse warriors, Tomahas and Tiloukaikt, entered the Whitmans' kitchen. Tiloukaikt had lost three

An artist's depiction of Marcus Whitman's death, more dramatic than accurate — Narcissa was not present at the time of her husband's death

Tomahas and Tiloukaikt,
Cayuse warriors

children to the white man's disease. When Marcus appeared, they shot him, then hacked him to death with a tomahawk.

At the sound of the fight, more Cayuse attacked the other people at the mission, killing eleven and taking forty-seven as hostages. Narcissa was among the dead, shot through a window. Her last words were a prayer for her adopted children: "Lord, save these little ones."

The captives were eventually released, including four of the trail orphans that Narcissa had prayed for. A pioneer army pursued the Cayuse until five warriors—including Tomahas and Tiloukaikt—turned themselves in so that the rest of the tribe would not be hunted down.

Before he was hanged for murder, Tiloukaikt was asked why he had surrendered. His answer showed that he had learned more from Narcissa and Marcus Whitman than they had thought.

"Did not your missionaries teach us that Christ died to save his people?" the warrior said. "So we die to save *our* people."

Mariano Guadalupe Vallejo

On March 16, 1846, Mariano Guadalupe Vallejo joined a small group of prominent Mexican citizens in Monterey, near San Francisco, to discuss the future of California.

Like the other men gathered at the meeting, Vallejo believed that Mexico was no longer capable of holding on to California, its northernmost province. Ignoring Mexican boundaries, Russia had maintained a fort less than a hundred miles up the coast from San Francisco. English fur companies from Oregon trapped and traded in northern California without asking Mexican permission. Foreign merchants controlled the businesses in Los Angeles and Monterey. And nearly three thousand Americans had crossed the Sierra Nevada into the Sacramento Valley to start farms, often in defiance of Mexican law.

Five years earlier, Vallejo had warned authorities in Mexico City to send troops and more Mexican settlers, or they would lose California. "Excuse this burst of feeling in a soldier," he wrote, "when he sees the treasure being stolen."

But not much had been done, and now the leading Californios (as the Mexicans born in California called themselves) could not agree on what steps to take next. One man favored asking France to annex California. Another suggested England. Still others called for a separate California republic—free not only from European nations, but from Mexico and the United States as well.

To rely any longer upon Mexico to govern and defend us would be idle and absurd. Why should we shrink from incorporating ourselves with the United States?

— *Mariano Vallejo*

Vallejo had a different suggestion. California should split off from Mexico, he said, and negotiate a peaceful annexation with the United States, "the happiest and freest nation in the world, destined soon to be the most wealthy and powerful."

Thinking of such a future, Vallejo said, "I feel nothing but pleasure." In less than three months, however, he would feel just the opposite.

•◆• •◆• •◆•

Vallejo belonged to one of the oldest and proudest Spanish families in the New World. One of his ancestors had sailed with Columbus. Another had helped Cortés conquer Mexico. And in the 1770s, his father had come north as a soldier to help Spain colonize the coast of California.

Vallejo, too, was trained for leadership. Besides Spanish, he learned English, French, and Latin. At age fourteen, he worked for the colonial governor and drew up the documents transferring California to Mexico after Mexico's independence from Spain in 1821. A year later, he became a soldier, and by the time he was twenty, he was leading an army against Indian uprisings.

In 1833, Vallejo was named military commander of northern California. He established himself at Sonoma to keep the Russians and the British

Vallejo's ranch house at Petaluma

and American fur trappers from encroaching even farther into Mexican territory.

Soon he was one of the largest landowners in the entire province of California. Some 250,000 acres—most of the Sonoma Valley—belonged to him. On his sprawling *rancho* grazed twenty-four thousand sheep, eight

Vaqueros lasso a grizzly bear.

thousand horses, and fifty thousand cattle—animals that the Spanish had brought from the Old World to the West.

Nearly everything we now associate with western ranching began with the Spanish and Mexicans. Vallejo's vaqueros (cowboys, both Mexican and Indian) were expert horsemen. They carried a rope called a *lazo* or lariat and wore broad-brimmed hats for shade from the sun and leather *chaparreras* (chaps) to protect their legs from cactus and thorny bushes.

Once a year, when it was time to bring in the cattle for branding and market, they held a roundup, called a rodeo. This was a great social event,

A Californio horse race

which included dances and parties, bullfights, horse races, and competitions between the vaqueros to display their skills. The Californios also enjoyed placing a bull and a grizzly bear in a ring and betting on which one would survive.

The cattle provided meat, but more important to Vallejo and the other ranchers were the cowhides, which were shipped around the world to factories that turned the leather into shoes and other goods. The fat, or tallow, from a cow's carcass was also exported, for use in making soap and candles.

The wealth of Vallejo and the other big landowners was based on Native American labor. Some of the Indian workers were captives who

I have two servants for myself. Four or five grind the corn. . . . Six or seven serve in the kitchen. Five or six are constantly busy washing the clothes of the children and servants. And nearly a dozen are required to attend to the sewing and spinning.

— Benicia Vallejo

had been taken in raids. Others were paid in food and clothing. Though technically free, they were under the absolute control of the landowner, like serfs in medieval Europe. Vallejo had his own private army of forty men and hundreds of Native American workers. "Each one of my children has a servant who has no other duty than to care for him or her," said Vallejo's wife, Benicia, mother of his sixteen children. Benicia herself had more than three dozen servants to help run her household.

Vallejo was renowned for his hospitality. Visiting dignitaries and businessmen from Europe often stayed at his large hacienda. A writer visiting from New England noted that Vallejo was "the most popular among the Americans and English of any man in California." In 1837, one of his sis-

Many wealthy Californios relied on Indian labor, as seen in this painting of a Monterey rancho by Alfred Sully.

ters married an American living in California, and for several years Vallejo and his new brother-in-law celebrated the American holiday of July Fourth with parties that lasted several days. At one of them, Vallejo gave a memorable speech in praise of George Washington and the American people.

"The Yankees are a wonderful people—wonderful!" he said. "Wherever they go, they make improvements."

By the spring of 1846, after Mexico City had repeatedly ignored his suggestions for asserting greater control over California, Vallejo decided that the best alternative would be to join the United States. "When we join our fortunes to hers, we shall not become subjects but fellow citizens, possessing all the rights of the people of the United States, and choosing our own federal and local rulers," he told the other Californios. "California will grow strong and flourish, and her people will be prosperous, happy, and free."

Vallejo with his daughters and granddaughters

Three months later, in the early morning of June 14, 1846, there was a loud knock on the door of Vallejo's house in Sonoma. A large group of strangers—mostly American trappers and settlers—demanded that Vallejo, as commander of northern California, surrender to them. They flew a flag decorated with a picture of a grizzly bear and said they were declaring California a republic—the Bear Flag Republic. They tied him to a chair and told him he was under arrest.

The bear flag

This was not the peaceful annexation he had hoped for. By the time Vallejo was released in August, the Bear Flag Revolt had been overwhelmed by the Mexican-American War. The United States Navy had landed in San Francisco. American troops had taken New Mexico and were marching into Mexico itself. When the fighting stopped in September of 1847, not only California but all of the Southwest belonged to the United States.

And soon after that, when gold was discovered in California, thousands upon thousands of Americans swarmed in. Before the Mexican-American War in 1846, about six thousand Californios had made up the non-Indian population of California. But by 1850, only one year after the gold rush, more than ninety thousand Americans had arrived, far outnumbering the Californios.

These legal thieves, clothed in the robes of law, took from us our lands and our houses, and without the least scruple enthroned themselves in our homes like so many powerful kings. For them existed no law but their own will.

— Mariano Vallejo

At first Vallejo adjusted to the new order of things. He helped write the state of California's constitution and was elected to its first senate. But like the other Californios he soon found himself and his old way of life overwhelmed. Lawsuits and illegal squatters steadily reduced his holdings—from a quarter of a million acres down to fewer than three hundred. His ranch and his wealth were lost. His people were viewed as "foreigners," and his culture was ridiculed.

As he grew older, he often felt betrayed by his American friends. "What a difference between the present time and those that preceded the Americans," he said. "If the Californios could all gather together to breathe a

An aging Mariano Vallejo, near his house in Sonoma, after losing most of his vast estate

lament, it would reach Heaven as a moving sigh which would cause fear and consternation in the Universe! What misery!"

But he never lost his sense of pride about his family and his people. The Spanish and Mexicans had already built their own society in the West, he wrote near the end of his life, "while General Washington was carrying on the war of the Revolution.

"We were the pioneers of the Pacific Coast," he said. "I had my day. It was a proud one."

William Swain

In April of 1849, the Missouri frontier towns of Independence and St. Joseph were jammed with thousands of wagons, mules, and oxen — and nearly thirty-five thousand men waiting impatiently for the spring rains to end and the soggy prairies to dry out so that their wagon trains could head west. Gold had been discovered in California, and the greatest human stampede in the nation's history was about to begin.

One of the men eager to set out was William Swain, a twenty-seven-year-old farmer from Youngstown, New York. Like all the others who called themselves forty-niners, Swain had read newspaper stories about people finding more than a hundred dollars a day in gold, simply by sifting through the rock and sand of California's rivers. It seemed like an easy way to make a lot of money, fast.

Despite the worries and objections of his wife, Sabrina, Swain had left their farm, promising to be back in a year's time with ten thousand dollars' worth of gold dust in his bag. Moving by steamboat, train, and riverboat, he had reached Independence—one thousand miles from his home, wife, and baby daughter—in less than a month.

But now the vast distances of the West lay ahead of him. He would have to travel nearly two thousand more miles, at the pace of a walking ox, before he could even *start* looking for gold. The journey would take half a year and would leave him wondering whether he should ever have left home at all.

At first, gold was easy to find. This man's nugget weighed eight pounds and was worth close to two thousand dollars.

•◆•　•◆•　•◆•

Swain's wagon train covered only eight miles the first day. His group called itself the Wolverine Rangers and painted the name on its wagon tops with axle grease. Other groups also displayed nicknames and mottoes—"Rough and Ready," "Wild Yankee," and "Never Say Die." There were sixty-three men in the Wolverine Rangers, including two doctors and two ministers, as well as carpenters, blacksmiths, tailors, and farmers like Swain.

Each man had contributed one hundred dollars to buy 18 covered wagons, 9 tents, 108 oxen, 10 milk cows, 4 ponies, and supplies. They had elected their leader and had agreed on rules they would follow during their long journey. "They are men of good habits," Swain wrote to his wife. "They are not to travel on the Sabbath and are to have preaching that day."

They broke their rule about traveling on Sunday after only two weeks. Wagon trains stretched ahead and behind them as far as the eye could see. No one wanted to be the last to reach California. And with so

Sabrina Swain

•◆•

many animals on the march, finding good grass for grazing became more difficult the farther back in line a wagon train was.

There were new experiences every mile. A buffalo herd passed in the distance, and the men chased it — for excitement and for meat, which Swain called "the sweetest and tenderest I have ever eaten."

Dear Sabrina,
Take care of yourself, my dear, for I am coming back again with a pocket full of rocks!

Yours truly, William

He watched in wonder as a summer thunderstorm moved steadily toward them on the open plains. Then hail started falling. "The air was literally *filled* with balls of ice from the size of a walnut to that of a goose egg," he wrote. Two wagons were damaged, and the men suffered bruises and cuts on their heads and backs. But they filled their buckets with hailstones, which provided cool ice water for the rest of the hot day.

There were Indians on the lands they crossed, and many of the Easterners were afraid of them at first. But fears of Indian raids proved groundless. Some tribes sold the emigrants bacon, beef, and vegetables, repaired their wagons, and built bridges over rivers for a price. During the gold rush, more men died from drowning or by an accident with their own guns than at the hands of Indians.

Disease was the biggest threat, especially cholera, which caused high fever, severe diarrhea, and often a painful death. Swain got sick in early June and was lucky to recover. But more than fifteen hundred other forty-niners died that summer and were buried in shallow graves along the trail. The disease spread from the wagon trains to Indian tribes and killed even more; half of the Cheyenne perished from it.

By July 4, Swain had crossed the prairies and reached Fort Laramie, a trading post in what is now Wyoming and the last stop before the mountains. There, many emigrants learned that their wagons were too heavy for the long, dry climb into the Rockies. Soon the trail was littered for miles with iron stoves, boxes, barrels, trunks of clothes, even the picks and shovels they knew they would need in California. Oxen and mules

died from exhaustion and bad water, and the air was filled with a hideous stench from the dead animals rotting in the sun.

After the mountains came the deserts of Nevada. In late September Swain's group grew worried that they wouldn't reach the Sierra Nevada before snows closed the high passes. Someone told them of a shortcut called Lassen's Cutoff, and they decided to take it. It turned out to be a big mistake.

First they had to cross the parched Black Rock Desert, traveling at night to escape the heat. Then they entered the Sierras, where wagons broke down and oxen died. They reached the tops of the mountains in early October, only to learn that the "shortcut" had brought them to northern California instead of the goldfields. They were no closer to their goal, and now it began to snow.

The Wolverine Rangers broke up into smaller groups and struggled on. Swain now carried only a change of clothes, his wallet, a few days' provi-

Dear George,

There was some talk between us of your coming to this country. For God's sake think not of it. Stay at home.

— William Swain

sions, and his Bible. He waded through drifts two feet deep, saw grizzly bear tracks on the trailside, and tied his clothes to his shoulders to keep them dry while fording icy rivers. Finally, on November 8, he reached a California settlement and sat down to write a letter to his brother.

"Dear George," he began. "There was some talk between us of your coming to this country. For God's sake think not of it. Stay at home."

By late 1849, when Swain arrived in California, the hills swarmed with prospectors.

Getting to California, he said, was "the hardest job I ever had." But now he had made it and was ready to start collecting all that easy gold he had heard about. His brother didn't need to come, he said, "for if my health is spared, I can get enough for both of us."

Like most of the other forty-niners who had taken the overland route, William Swain was stunned by the surprise waiting for him in California. The gold region's riverbanks were already even more crowded with men than the trail west had been. Some eighty-nine thousand men had arrived that year, chasing the same dream. Many had come by ship instead of overland. Besides Americans, there were gold seekers from Mexico, China, South America, and Europe. More were arriving every day. And by late 1849, when Swain arrived, most of the easy pickings were over.

In the early days after the first discovery, all a prospector needed was a pick, a shovel, and a tin pan to dig some gravel in the riverbank, put it in his pan, and sift out the gold. Others used a device called a rocker, about four feet long, that did the same thing only with larger amounts of gravel.

But now they would need to dig deeper and wash even more gravel, often to get smaller amounts of gold. Teams of men used "Long Toms"—

Miners often used rockers called "Long Toms" to sift gold from the gravel.

If there is no gold, we shall be off to another place, for there is an abundance of gold here, and if we are blessed with health, we are determined to have a share of it.

— *William Swain*

rockers that were fifteen feet long. Others built dams or wooden channels, called flumes, to divert the rushing waters so the miners could get to the river bottoms. The days of the single prospector working alone were already ending.

Swain went into a partnership with several other men to stake out a claim along the Feather River. They built a small cabin, started on a dam and flume, and learned how backbreaking the work could be. The forty-niners called their areas "the diggings," because digging is what they did, day in and day out.

"George," Swain wrote home to his brother, "I tell you this mining among the mountains is a dog's life."

He had a few successes—thirty five dollars worth of gold one day, fifty-one dollars another, and ninety-two dollars on a particularly good one. More often he made less, or nothing at all.

George Swain

And most of what he earned went to pay for food and supplies, sold at wildly expensive prices in the mining camps. An onion cost a dollar, eggs were fifty cents apiece, a jar of pickles eight dollars, and a bottle of rum twenty dollars.

In March Swain paid two dollars for his mail to be brought from San Francisco, the closest post office. It was the first letter to reach him from home in more than a year. He wrote back that it would take him longer than expected to reach his goal of ten thousand dollars and that, like most of the other forty-niners, he was homesick. But he was keeping his promise of reading the Bible, staying out of trouble, and keeping his spirits up, though he couldn't say the same for many of the others. "Drinking has become very prevalent, swearing a habitual custom," he wrote, "and gambling has no equal in the annals of history."

If the spring rains would only let up, he said, they could "get into the bed of the river and know what is there. If there is no gold, we shall be off to another place." But the rains kept falling. Swain traveled south to the Yuba River, then north to another, then back to his claim when the weather cleared, but made only two dollars a day for his trouble.

By June he had chills and fevers from spending so much time in cold rivers. He had lost weight and was feeling weak. He sold his share in his partnership for seven hundred dollars and looked for other sites without much success.

Thousands who one month ago felt certain that their chances were sure for a fortune are at this time without money or any chance of any, and hundreds of dollars in debt. Certainly such a turn of fortune is enough to sicken the heart of any man. — William Swain

In August he wrote that nine out of ten miners had seen "their bright daydreams of golden wealth vanish like dreams of night." By October he was sick again and wanted to go home. But he was worried that, after all the reports of easy money in California, his family and friends would consider him a failure if he returned without anything close to his ten thousand dollars.

Then a letter arrived from his brother.

"Above all, keep your courage up," it said. "If you fail there, you are not to blame. You have friends who will meet you just as cordially unsuccessful as successful—and more so, for we are sure you have suffered, suffered, suffered. To tell the plain truth, I wish most sincerely you were at home, no matter if you haven't got a single cent."

On November 10, 1850, William Swain stood on the crowded docks of San Francisco, a city that had grown from several hundred people to thirty thousand residents in the short time since gold had been discovered.

Dear Friends,
Here I am in this city on my way home, thank God.
I have made up my mind that I have got enough of
California and am coming home as fast as I can.

— *William Swain*

The harbor was jammed with ships bringing in still more hopeful prospectors and supplies to be sold to the growing surge of miners.

For Swain, it had the same air of excitement he'd experienced in Independence, Missouri, a year and a half earlier. Even though he had only five hundred dollars' worth of gold dust in his bag, he was going home. And he was not alone. Homesick

Masts of hundreds of ships lined the harbor of San Francisco, the growing hub of the gold rush.

William Swain, long after his return from California, sitting amidst his family at his home in upstate New York

and disappointed that gold prospecting had turned out to be harder work and less profitable than they had expected, most of the forty-niners eventually returned home, too.

A boat took Swain to Panama, where he crossed over the mountains and jungles to the Atlantic Ocean, then boarded another ship to New York City. By February 1851 he was in Youngstown, hugging his wife and daughter and shaking hands with the brother whose letter had given him the courage to come back.

Swain and his brother went into business together and became the biggest peach growers in Niagara County, New York. But at night, when the work was done, Swain would sit on the porch and tell his family stories of his adventures crossing the West and pursuing a dream of easy gold in California.

"John Chinaman" Builds a Railroad

In 1865 a great race across the West was in progress.

The first railroad to go all the way from the Missouri River to the Pacific Ocean was being built. No one had ever tried before to lay track over such vast distances—1,775 miles filled with mountains, deserts, and sometimes hostile Indians. It was a huge task, requiring the resources of two different companies. The Central Pacific line began in Sacramento, California, heading east. The Union Pacific line started at Omaha, Nebraska, pushing west. Whichever company built the most railroad track by the time they met would get the most money—and glory. And in early 1865, it looked like the Central Pacific might not get much of either one.

The company had been working for nearly two years and so far had laid only thirty-six miles of track. Even worse, directly in front of the Central Pacific's path lay the towering Sierras, far more of a challenge than the rolling Great Plains that the Union Pacific had to cross. As if that wasn't enough of a handicap, the Central Pacific had only six hundred of the five thousand workers it needed to get over the mountains. Many of the laborers it hired kept leaving to search for gold and silver.

Charles Crocker, the company's construction boss, realized something drastic had to be done. He decided to hire Chinese workers.

Others tried to talk him out of it. The Chinese were too small for such work, these skeptics said, and had no experience in building railroads. And because of discrimination against people who spoke a different language and practiced a different religion, they added, other workers might quit their jobs.

Give the Chinese a chance, Crocker answered. It turned out to be the best decision he ever made.

Charles Crocker

•◆• •◆• •◆•

Crocker started with a small crew of fifty Chinese men. Other people made fun of them, but they soon proved themselves to be hard workers, so Crocker hired more. Eventually eleven thousand Chinese—90 percent of the company's labor force, and one quarter of all the Chinese living in the United States at the time—would work for the Central Pacific.

Unfortunately, almost no first-hand accounts (diaries, letters, or memoirs) from individual workers exist. Most Americans referred to them simply as "coolies" or "John Chinaman." But we know they

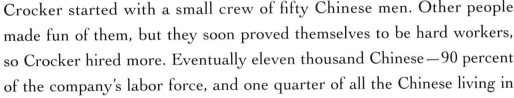

The rugged mountains look like stupendous ant-hills. They swarm with Chinese, shoveling, wheeling, carting, drilling and blasting rocks and earth, while their eyes stare out from under immense basket hats in shape and size like umbrellas.

— THE RAILROAD RECORD

The Chinese used picks and shovels . . .

came to the West for the same reason so many other people from other countries had come—they wanted a chance to get ahead in life. Some had arrived during the gold rush, when leaflets circulated in China calling California the "Gold Mountain." Others were fleeing political revolution and famine at home. Even more came when Charles Crocker recognized their skills and work habits and began recruiting them directly from China to fill his growing need for workers.

and explosives to make a path for the railroad.

Building a railroad was dangerous, backbreaking labor. To clear a smooth road for the rails, giant redwood trees had to be cut down by hand and their huge stumps dug and blasted out of the ground. Huge bridges were built across deep canyons. Five hundred kegs of blasting powder were used each day to make cuts through the foothills.

When the line reached a cliff of solid rock called Cape Horn, nearly straight up and down, two thousand feet above a raging river, the Chinese were told to carve a ledge across it wide enough for a train. Men were lowered over the cliff in small baskets, swaying in the wind over the canyon while they drilled holes in the rock. They set explosives in the holes and then signaled to be yanked up before the charge went off.

"John Chinaman" did it all, and did it well—even though the Chinese earned less than other workers. Americans and Chinese both were paid about thirty dollars a month. But while the others got free food and shelter from the company, the Chinese had to provide for their own. They ate fish, bamboo sprouts, rice, vegetables, and fruit, and drank tea made with boiled water. This kept them healthier than the other workers, who often got sick from bad water and a diet of only beef and potatoes. Crocker

A Chinese camp

Having to cut tunnels through solid granite slowed the pace to eight inches a day.

noticed that the Chinese were cleaner, too, because their custom was to give themselves sponge baths every day.

They worked in groups of twenty, usually under the supervision of a clan leader from their home village. Their main goal was to earn money to send back to their families in China. They knew that some westerners, opposed to Chinese immigration, were hoping that they'd fail. But "a lazy one does not exist," said one American who watched them at their job. Others began calling them "Crocker's pets."

By the winter of 1866, they neared the tops of the mountains, seven thousand feet above sea level, and the work got even tougher. They had to dig fifteen tunnels through granite so hard that it quickly wore out their drills. It took them an entire day just to move ahead eight inches. Crocker was told that Cornish miners from England were the world's best tunnelers, so he hired some to see if they could go faster. "We measured the work every Sunday morning," he said, "and the Chinamen, without fail, always outmeasured" the competition.

Heavy snows began to fall. Soon drifts towered over forty feet high. But the race across the West meant that the Central Pacific had to keep working. The Chinese dug out snow tunnels to live in that winter, with chimneys and air shafts reaching up through the deep drifts above them. Some men froze to death. Others were swept away by avalanches, and their bodies weren't found until the next spring, with their hands still frozen to their picks and shovels. No one kept a precise count, but at least 1,200 Chinese workers died as the Central Pacific pushed forward.

John Chinaman has broken down the great barrier at last and opened over it the greatest highway yet created for the march of commerce and civilization around the globe. —THE TERRITORIAL ENTERPRISE

*Despite heavy snows,
work went on.*

Then, in early 1868, they conquered the Sierras. "John Chinaman has broken down the great barrier at last and opened over it the greatest highway yet created for the march of commerce and civilization around the globe," reported the *Territorial Enterprise* newspaper.

*A funeral for one of the
many Chinese workers who
died building the railroad*

But now the workers faced a new challenge: the searing deserts of Nevada. It was flatter, but there was little or no water, no trees to make railroad ties, and plenty of scorpions and tarantulas to make life miserable. Even worse, the summer temperatures rose to 120 degrees. Men collapsed from heat and exhaustion, yet they pushed on—372 miles across Nevada by the end of 1868.

A crew moves along the new track on a handcart.

Meanwhile, the Union Pacific had been racing across the plains. One day, their mostly Irish workers laid six miles of track. The Central Pacific's Chinese topped that with seven miles. The Union Pacific answered with seven and three-quarter miles.

Charles Crocker bragged that his crews could do what no railroad builders had ever done before—lay ten miles of track in a single day. The Union Pacific's boss bet ten thousand dollars that it was impossible.

At sunrise on April 28, 1869, a whistle blew, and five thousand Central Pacific men went to work. Each one had his own assignment. Some

Chinese workers at Promontory, Utah

placed the wooden railroad ties across the roadbed. Others moved the heavy iron rails (each one weighed six hundred pounds) onto handcars, which men and horses pulled to the end of the line. Specialists called ironmen lifted the rails and put them carefully on the ties. (The eight ironmen were big Irish workers, but the others were Chinese.) Then men drove in spikes and bolted on connecting plates to hold the rails in place, while tamping crews smoothed the roadbed out again so that the rail line would lay flat and straight.

No one could believe how fast and efficiently the Central Pacific laborers could work. The railroad line was moving forward as fast as a man could walk!

At sunset, the whistle blew again, and the sweating, exhausted workers stopped. They had put down 25,800 ties and two million pounds of iron rail, driven 28,160 spikes and used 14,080 bolts. And from the point they had started in the morning, they had come exactly 10 miles and 56 feet.

The two rail lines were officially joined at Promontory, Utah, on May 10, 1869.

Crocker had won his bet. And "John Chinaman," whom everyone had once scorned, had set a record of railroad building that no one has beaten to this day.

On May 10, 1869, the Central Pacific and Union Pacific finally met, and a golden spike was driven to mark the spot. More than three years earlier, when the race had begun, people assumed that the junction would occur near the California-Nevada state line, since the Union Pacific did not have the rugged Sierras to cross.

But instead, the ceremony took place at Promontory Summit, in Utah. Crocker's Chinese crews had built nearly five hundred more miles of track than anyone had expected.

It was a great day of celebration—for the West and for the nation. At last, people could travel by train from the Atlantic to the Pacific.

"John Chinaman," however, was not given much credit for the achievement. Many people still

I wish to call to your minds that the early completion of this railroad we have built has been in large measure due to that poor, despised class of laborers called the Chinese, to the fidelity and industry they have shown.
— *Charles Crocker*

believed that the Chinese were too different, that they took jobs away from Americans, that the nation would be better off if they went back to China.

Charles Crocker knew better. On the day the golden spike was driven, he said, "I wish to call to your minds that the early completion of this railroad we have built has been in large measure due to that poor, despised class of laborers called the Chinese, to the fidelity and industry they have shown."

Teddy Blue Abbott

In 1871, when Edward C. "Teddy Blue" Abbott was ten years old, his family moved from England to a homestead in Nebraska. Soon after they arrived, his father needed to buy some cattle for their farm and took young Teddy with him on the train down to Texas to buy a small herd.

"I was the poorest, sickliest little kid you ever saw, all eyes, no flesh on me whatever," Teddy Blue remembered. A doctor had suggested that some fresh air might improve Teddy's health. So his father let him ride along on the trail drive all the way back from Texas to Nebraska.

Teddy Blue camped out under the stars at night and rode a pony he called Pete every day, taking care of the extra horses as the herd moved north. The work, the exercise, and the open air made him stronger and healthier.

By the time he reached Nebraska, ten-year-old Teddy Blue had made what would be the biggest decision of his life. He didn't want to be a farmer like his father.

His first trail drive "made a cowboy out me," he said. "Nothing could have changed me after that."

•◆• •◆• •◆•

That decision caused trouble between Teddy Blue and his dad. "I was out on the range, running wild, when other boys were in school," he said of his teenage years.

He raced his pony Pete against the horses of some Pawnee Indians living in the area, and he once tried to sneak away from home to join the tribe on a buffalo hunt. He watched as some horse thieves were hanged, then showed his friends how it was done by stringing up his family's prize turkey. And he took jobs herding neighbors' cattle for a dollar-fifty per cow every six months, earning a total of twenty-nine dollars one year.

"I never had a boyhood," he said. "I was a man by the time I was twelve years old—doing a man's work, living with men, having men's ideas."

When he was eighteen, he left home for good. For the next four years, he stayed on the trail, living in his saddle.

The late 1870s and early 1880s were the final years of the big cattle drives that had started in the West after the Civil War. Herds of long-horns were moved from Texas to places like Kansas, where railroads shipped the cattle east for the beef desired by people in the growing cities; or to Indian reservations, to feed the tribes that had once relied on buffalo for food; or to Nebraska, Wyoming, and Montana, to start huge cattle ranches where the buffalo once roamed.

Lots of times I have ridden around the herd, with lightning playing and thunder muttering in the distance, when the air was so full of electricity that I would see it flashing on the horns of the cattle.

— *Teddy Blue Abbott*

A cowboy's life was far different from the way Hollywood movies would later portray it. There was not much romance, even less gunplay, and hardly any Indian fighting. "A cowboy with two guns is all movie stuff, and so is this business of a gun on each hip," Teddy Blue said later in life. Gambling and drinking were often prohibited out on the trail. Instead, it was day after day of riding a horse and working with cattle.

Riding "the drags" was a dusty job.

Each cowboy had an assignment as he drove a herd north—slowly, so the cattle wouldn't lose weight and bring less money when they reached their destination. Usually two cowboys rode in front, on the "point;" on the sides, two rode on the "swing," then two more a little farther back on the "flank." Two "worked the drags," riding behind the two thousand cattle. Each outfit also had a cook, a wrangler, who took care of the extra horses, and a trail boss, who was in charge.

No cowboy liked working the drags. "I have seen them come off herd with the dust half an inch deep on their hats and thick as fur in their eyebrows and mustaches, and if they shook their head or you tapped their cheek, it would fall off them in showers," Teddy Blue said. "They would go to the water barrel at the end of the day and rinse their mouths and cough and spit and bring up that black stuff out of their throats. But you couldn't get it up out of your lungs."

Out on the open prairies, the cowboys were at the mercy of the weather. Sometimes they went days without water, and Teddy Blue learned that the worst thing to do is lick your lips—it just makes things worse. Other times, hail stones fell so hard that he had to hide under his saddle for protection.

"Lots of cowpunchers were killed by lightning," he said. "I was knocked off my horse by it twice. The first time, I saw a ball of fire coming toward me and felt something strike me on the head. When I came to, I was lying under old Pete and the rain was pouring down on my face."

If you wasn't singing, any little sound in the night— it might be just a horse shaking himself— could make [the cattle] leave the country; but if you were singing, they wouldn't notice it. — Teddy Blue Abbott

Storms—and sudden noises at night—could stampede the cattle. That was the most dangerous time for the cowboys, who tried to turn the herd into a circle and slow it down. "It was riding at a dead run in the dark, with cut banks [gullies] and prairie dog holes all around you," Teddy Blue remembered, "not knowing if the next jump would land you in a shallow grave."

He lost three friends in stampedes like that. Two died in falls, and one was trampled by the rampaging cattle. By comparison, Teddy Blue

Trail herds often contained as many as two thousand cattle.

witnessed only a few gunfights in his career and never saw anyone shot to death.

"But when you add it all up, I believe the worst hardship we had on the trail was loss of sleep," he said. "There was never enough sleep." The workday began before sunrise and didn't end until after nine o'clock,

On the trail, cowboys slept under the open sky.

when the herd was brought to a halt. Then, during the night, pairs of cowboys took turns every two hours riding around the herd to make sure the cattle were safe. Often they sang to the cows and steers to soothe them.

Five hours' worth of sleep was considered a lot; most often cowboys got much less. To keep awake at work, Teddy Blue and the others sometimes rubbed tobacco juice in their eyes. "It was like rubbing them with fire," he remembered.

Like Teddy Blue, most of the cowboys were young and small. Small, because a heavy cowboy was hard on the horse he rode. Young, because the work hours were so long and so hard, the food on the trail so bad (usually just beans and bread), and the pay so low (Teddy Blue got just thirty dollars a month) that older men were uninterested. Many cowboys quit after just one trail drive. Others were hunched and crippled for life because of the constant pounding their bodies received from riding over rough ground every day.

In person the cowboys were mostly medium-sized men, as a heavy man was hard on horses; quick and wiry; and as a rule good-natured; in fact, it did not pay to be anything else. In character, their like never was or will be again.
— Teddy Blue Abbott

In 1883 Teddy Blue went on his last drive — 1,500 miles from San Antonio, Texas, all the way to the Yellowstone River in Montana. There he left the trail to work on a big ranch.

For years, homesteaders had been moving into the West, starting farms and passing laws to stop cattle drives from coming through and ruining their crops. And there were now more railroads, which could move cattle across long distances faster and cheaper than driving them on foot.

The days of long trail drives were ending — not just for Teddy Blue but everywhere in the West. "I had stopped drifting and didn't want to wander anymore," he said. "I was a Montana cowboy now."

Teddy Blue and friends, after his last trail drive

For Teddy Blue and other cowboys, ranch life was a little easier than being on the trail. They slept in bunkhouses instead of on the open ground, and the food was usually better. But the work was still hard enough. There were roundups at least once a year, when the calves were branded and some cattle shipped to market. Cowboys still spent long months far from town and other people. The pay was still low. Life was still anything but romantic.

In parts of Montana, Wyoming, and the Dakotas, as well as other pockets of the West, there were still huge sections of unfenced government-owned land, referred to as the open range. To the big ranchers it was free grass, and they turned their cattle loose on it to roam all year. Many rich

On the ranch, cowboys slept in a bunkhouse.

easterners and Europeans invested, lured by the promise of sure and easy profits.

Then came the winter of 1886. Where Teddy Blue was working, it started snowing in November and didn't stop for a month. January was the coldest anyone could remember. Cowboys were sent out to check on the cattle, which were starving and scattering from the blizzard winds.

"Think of riding all day in a blinding snowstorm, the temperature fifty or sixty below zero, and no dinner," Teddy Blue recalled. "Here were the clothes I wore: two pairs of wool socks, a pair of moccasins, a pair of Dutch socks that came up to my knees, a pair of government overshoes, two suits of heavy underwear, pants, overalls, chaps, and a big heavy shirt. I got a pair of woman's stockings and cut the feet out and made sleeves. I wore wool gloves, and great big heavy mittens, a blanket-lined sourdough overcoat, and a great big sealskin cap." Still, it was hard to keep warm.

All across the Great Plains that winter, the unsheltered, helpless cattle began to die. Some, too weak to stand, were simply blown over by the fierce wind. Others, their feet frozen into the ice, died where they stood, looking like statues.

When the snow and ice finally melted the next spring, the cowboys rode out again. Dead animals were everywhere, hundreds of thousands of them. Some were sprawled across the hillsides and along fence lines. Others were heaped at the bottom of big gullies, called coulees, where they had been trapped by the snow. "The weather was hot, and the dead cattle in the coulees—you'd come across little bunches of ten or fifteen or twenty of them piled up," Teddy Blue said. "Phew! I can smell them yet."

After the blizzards of 1886/1887, most ranchers gathered in their herds for winter.

Now he witnessed the closing of another chapter in the history of American cowboys. Many of the open range ranches failed, and the wealthy investors pulled out. More fences went up. Instead of leaving their cattle free to roam, ranchers would have to gather them in and feed them during the winter.

They were intensely loyal to the outfit they were working for and would fight to the death for it. They would follow their wagon boss through hell and never complain. Living that kind of life, [cowboys] were bound to be wild and brave.

— Teddy Blue Abbott

Teddy Blue married a woman who was half-Indian and took up a homestead, where they raised eight children. "Nothing was like it used to be," he said. "From now on I wasn't a cowpuncher anymore."

Teddy Blue lived to age seventy-eight. Before he died, in 1939, he became concerned that Hollywood movies weren't portraying cowboys accurately, showing gunfights and Indian attacks instead of cows, horses, and hard work. "They're like these cowboy songs I've heard over the radio," he said of the movies. "All fixed up and not the way we used to sing them at all." So he told his life story to a writer, in hopes that a part of the real history of the West would never be forgotten.

"Cowpunching as we knew it is a thing of the past," he said. "Only a few of us are left now. The rest have left the wagon and gone ahead across the big divide, looking for a new range. I hope they find good water and plenty of grass. But wherever they are is where I want to go."

Teddy Blue Abbott
in the late 1930s

Uriah and Mattie Oblinger

In the fall of 1872, Uriah Oblinger went out with a horse and plow to begin work at his brand-new homestead on the treeless prairies of Nebraska. For centuries buffalo had roamed and grazed on these grasslands, and the thick sod had never before been turned by a plow. The noise of the matted grass roots tearing loose from the soil sounded like the opening of a giant zipper.

As he plowed his field to prepare for planting, Oblinger saved the top layer of sod for another purpose. His wife Mattie and their daughter, Ella, were still on their rented farm back in Onward, Indiana, waiting for Uriah to prepare a new home for them in the West. He cut the strips of sod into chunks—called "Nebraska bricks"—and began stacking them. Slowly he made four walls, with spaces for a door and a window. Then he covered the walls with a roof of sod that still had grass growing on top of it.

It was small and dark and made entirely of dirt—but it was all his, and he couldn't have been prouder. At last he was ready for his family. "The longer I stay here, the better I like it," he wrote Mattie, telling her to bring Ella and come to Nebraska.

You can see just as far as you please here, and almost every foot in sight can be plowed.

— *Uriah Oblinger*

Like millions of other western homesteaders in the 1870s, Uriah Oblinger was an optimist. Even through the small window of a sod house, the future looked bright. Under the new Homestead Act, passed by Congress in 1862, to help settle the West and to make more Americans property owners, the federal government was offering 160 acres to anyone willing to pay ten dollars and work the land for five years.

For the Oblingers, homesteading meant that for the first time they could have their own land and build a better life for their growing family. But

Like the Oblingers, this family lived in a sod house built of "Nebraska bricks".

they would soon learn—as did many others—that homesteading could also mean constant labor, incredible hardship, and painful heartbreak.

•◆• •◆• •◆•

Uriah, Ella, and
Mattie Oblinger

In May of 1873, with one crate bearing all their possessions and a second crate filled with live chickens, Mattie and little Ella arrived in Nebraska and moved into the small "soddy" that Uriah had built. If Mattie was disappointed about living in a dirt house, she didn't complain. "I ripped our wagon sheet in two and have it around the sides" of the walls, she wrote to her parents. "It looks real swell."

Newcomers to the treeless plains discovered that the thick, earthen-walled sod houses kept them cooler in summer and warmer in winter than wood houses could. But their dirt ceilings and dirt floors made them harder to keep clean. "Mother disliked sweeping her floor with a hoe," one pioneer boy remembered. Another Nebraska girl joked: "There was running water in our sod house—it ran in through the roof every time it rained."

Soon the Oblingers settled into a routine common to most homesteaders. They ate what they raised. Uriah butchered a hog for meat and planted crops of wheat and barley in the fields. Mattie raised chickens for eggs and started a vegetable garden. Her main problems were rattlesnakes (Uriah killed two the first year) and gophers that ate her peas. Still, she grew squash, water-

At home in our house and a sod at that! … It is not quite so convenient as a nice frame, but I would as soon live in it as the cabins I have lived in. The only objection I have is that we have no floor yet.

— *Mattie Oblinger*

On the sweeping prairie, many homesteaders planted trees for shade and comfort.

melon, cucumbers, tomatoes, and corn. "We brought in beets just now that measured one foot in circumference," she boasted to her parents in a let-ter, "and potatoes almost as large as goose eggs."

After three years, they bought two cows. Ella cried for joy at the sight of them and the thought of fresh milk each day. She helped with the chores—feeding the chickens, gathering eggs, milking the cows, and scrubbing the tin dishes with sand (the Oblingers didn't have enough money to dig a well; they hauled water from a distant stream and saved it for more important uses than washing dishes).

The longer I stay here, the better I like it. They are mostly young families, just starting in life the same way as we are, and I find them very generous indeed. We will all be poor here together.

— Uriah Oblinger

Two more girls were born—Stella, then Maggie. Stella was one-and-a-half years old when Uriah took her by wagon on the thirty-two-mile trip to

Stella, Ella, and
Maggie Oblinger

Elk Creek, where he planned to cut some cottonwoods for fuel. She had never seen a tree before "and did not know what to make of the timber," her mother wrote. One year, the big attraction in the area was an evergreen Christmas tree at the one-room schoolhouse—something so unusual that Ella wrote to her grandparents in Indiana to tell them all about it. She also told them about the presents she and her sisters had received—a homemade calico dress, a book, a doll, and a string with candy and raisins on it.

Times were never easy. In 1874 grasshoppers descended on the plains in swarms so huge and thick that they darkened the midday sky. They devoured the crops. In 1876, they came again, followed by a prairie fire that swept through the area. Men plowed circles

A typical one-room
schoolhouse

around their houses to prevent the fire from jumping onto the roofs, but the schoolhouse burned down. Until a new one was built, the Oblinger girls attended school in a grain shed.

Other setbacks began driving many homesteaders off the land in discouragement. One August, Mattie Oblinger noted that her family hadn't had any meat since winter and that her neighbors were wearing grain sacks for clothes. Stacking wheat one afternoon, Uriah collapsed from heatstroke, and his recovery was slow. When the weather turned cold, the Oblingers burned cornstalks for fuel, because they

What a pleasure it is to work on one's own farm, for you can feel that it is yours and not for someone else.

— *Uriah Oblinger*

For all homesteaders, plowing and planting were hard work.

couldn't afford coal and wood was very scarce. Relatives sent them a barrelful of presents—clothes, chestnuts, dried apples, and cans of peaches, which the girls considered great delicacies.

But throughout the hard times, Uriah kept his spirits up. "What a pleasure it is to work on one's own farm," he wrote, "for you can feel that it is yours and not for someone else. I would rather live as we do than have to rent and have someone bossing us as we used to do."

Then, in February 1880, the worst tragedy of all struck the Oblingers. Pregnant with a fourth child, Mattie went into labor in the sod house. Neither she nor the baby survived the difficult childbirth. They were buried on the prairie.

Uriah had already met drought, grasshopper plagues, prairie fires, and every other adversity with hope and determination. But the death of Mattie and the baby seemed to break his optimistic spirit. It was several months before he could even bring himself to write home about how he and the three little girls were surviving on the frontier without a wife and mother.

"I try to bear the trouble cheerfully," he said, "though the task is hard at times. This season has not been a success with me in farming. Crops and prices are so poor that it is making times pretty close here, and my misfortunes during the past year have put me back badly. I hardly know how to manage."

He tried everything to keep the family and farm together—even rented his land and hired himself out with his prize horse to plow other people's fields, taking the girls along wherever he worked.

But in the end, faced with the prospect of sending his daughters away to be raised by different relatives, he gave up his homestead and returned to his parents' home back East, where he supported the children by working for the railroad and doing chores for other people.

His dream of a fresh start, farming his own land in the West, seemed to have ended in failure.

But Uriah Oblinger never gave up that dream. After marrying again, he moved his family back to Nebraska in 1883 and started all over on a new farm just one and a half miles from the one he had given up.

Uriah Oblinger in later years

He stayed in the West the rest of his life, raising Ella, Stella, and Maggie, along with three more daughters, with his new wife. He died in Nebraska in 1901, being cared for by Ella, who had first come to the plains with her mother, Mattie, so many years before, chasing their dream of a new life in the West.

Chief Joseph

In 1877 a young chief of the Nez Percés faced a terrible choice. He could sell and abandon his people's homeland in the beautiful Wallowa Mountains of northeastern Oregon. Or he could resist the demands of the U.S. government and go to war for the right to stay. He knew that a war with the United States would mean misery and death for many, both Indians and whites. But he also could not forget the promise he had made to his dying father six years earlier. "My son," the old man had said before passing on to the Spirit World, "a few years more, and the white men will be all around you. They have their eyes on this land. You must stop your ears whenever you are asked to sign a treaty selling your home. Never forget my dying words. This country holds your father's body. Never sell the bones of your father and mother."

The son's name was Hin-mah-too-yah-lat-kekht, or Thunder Rolling from the Mountains. But he was known to white people as Chief Joseph. And his constant attempts to remain true to his promises, while others ignored their own, would make him one of the most noble and respected Indian leaders in American history—as well as one of the most tragic.

•◆• •◆• •◆•

Of all the Indian peoples of the West, none had a longer record of unbroken friendship with the United States than the Nez Percés.

In 1805 they had met their first white men, the American explorers Lewis and Clark, and exchanged promises of peace. In 1836 they had welcomed the missionaries Henry and Eliza Spalding, who converted and baptized some of

You might as well expect the rivers to run backward as that any man who was born a free man should be contented penned up and denied liberty to go where he pleases.   — *Chief Joseph*

the tribe into Christianity. When their Cayuse neighbors rose up and massacred missionaries Marcus and Narcissa Whitman, the Nez Percés had protected the Spaldings. And in the 1850s, when other tribes in the Northwest went to war against American settlers and miners rushing onto their lands, the Nez Percés had refused to join in.

"It has always been the pride of the Nez Percés," Chief Joseph said later, "that they were the friends of the white men."

But in 1877, as Indian people all over the West were being forced onto reservations by the U.S. government, that friendship was put to the test. General Oliver O. Howard arrived to announce that Chief Joseph's Wallowa band had to leave their homes and move onto a reser-

General Oliver O. Howard and Chief Joseph

vation in Idaho, where the rest of the tribe already lived. White people were crowding into Oregon's Wallowa country, claiming that a government treaty permitted them to settle on Nez Percé land.

I said in my heart that, rather than have war, I would give up my country. I would give up my father's grave. I would give up everything rather than have the blood of white men upon the hands of my people.

— *Chief Joseph*

Joseph explained that the Wallowa Nez Percés had never signed a treaty selling their land to the United States. General Howard checked the documents, which showed that Chief Joseph was right, and asked Washington for a change in orders. But the word came back to clear the Wallowa of Indians, with or without a treaty. Howard made Chief Joseph a new offer—the U.S. government would pay for the land. When Joseph refused, stating that the law—and simple justice—was on his side, he was given a month to move his people to Idaho or troops would be sent to remove them by force.

The young chief, still in his thirties, now faced the hardest decision of his life. "I knew I had never sold my country," he said, "but I did not want bloodshed. I did not want my people killed. I did not want *anybody* killed.

The Nez Percés wanted peace but were skilled in battle.

I said in my heart that, rather than have war, I would give up my country. I would give up my father's grave. I would give up everything rather than have the blood of white men upon the hands of my people."

Joseph and the other chiefs reluctantly began moving their bands to the reservation. But a handful of young warriors, seeking revenge for the way their people had been treated, slipped away and murdered some white settlers. In response, Howard's soldiers attacked the Nez Percé camp, thinking they'd win an easy victory. Instead, on June 17, at the Battle of White Bird Canyon, the army lost thirty-four men and the Indians lost none.

The war that Joseph had tried so hard to avoid had now begun.

I have carried a heavy load on my back ever since I was a boy. I learned then that we were but few, while the white men were many. We were like deer. They were like grizzly bears.

— *Chief Joseph*

He and the other leaders decided to leave the region. In Montana, they thought, the white people would not bother them. And their friends the Crow would shelter them until a peace could be arranged in Idaho.

They set out at once for the long journey, hoping the soldiers would not pursue them. But Howard's soldiers kept after them. While still in Idaho, the Nez Percés had to fight three more battles against army troops—and won them all. "I have been in lots of scrapes," one army scout said, "but I never went up against anything like the Nez Percés in all my life."

In mid-July, the Indians started the hard climb through the rugged Bitterroot Mountains into Montana. There were about seven hundred people in the group. Only two hundred were warriors, though. The rest were women, children, and old people with their horse herds, tepees, and belongings. Still, they managed to move more quickly than Howard's men.

White settlers in Montana panicked at the news that a "war party" was headed their way. But Chief Joseph's people passed peacefully through the Bitterroot River valley, even paying for supplies as they went. After a month of hard traveling, they came to a grassy meadow

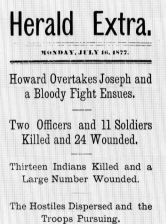

Herald Extra.

MONDAY, JULY 16, 1877.

Howard Overtakes Joseph and a Bloody Fight Ensues.

Two Officers and 11 Soldiers Killed and 24 Wounded.

Thirteen Indians Killed and a Large Number Wounded.

The Hostiles Dispersed and the Troops Pursuing.

called the Big Hole. The weary Indians decided that the soldiers were too far behind to worry about, and they set up their tepees, planning to rest for several days.

But at dawn the next morning, they were awakened by gunfire pouring into their village. A different army, sent from a Montana fort, had surprised them. Between sixty and ninety Nez Percés were killed—more than half of them women and children—before the soldiers were driven from the camp. Joseph led the surviving women and children to safety while the warriors counterattacked. They killed twenty-nine soldiers and wounded forty more.

Still grieving for their dead, the Nez Percés hurried south. Howard's army was right behind them once again. They turned east, directly toward Yellowstone National Park, which had been established five years earlier. As the Nez Percés swept through, they captured more than a dozen tourists. Most were released unharmed, but against the chiefs' orders, two were killed.

Meanwhile, more army troops had been dispatched from all over the West. Howard was sure that Joseph and his people were trapped in the park and could not escape. But they did and were still hoping to find refuge with their old allies the Crow near the Yellowstone River.

Independent Extra
Big Hole Battle.

Gibbon Makes a Desperate Fight and is Overpowered.

LOGAN & BRADLEY KILLED

Gibbon and three Lieutenants Wounded.

" Help! Help!! Send us all the Relief you. We are Cut off from Supplies."

Herald Extra.

HELENA, SUNDAY, JULY 29.

Joseph's Band Escaping by way of Henry's Lake.

DEER LODGE, July 29.—A letter from old Beaverhead Station says: Thirty or forty lodges of Indians are camped forty miles south of that place, on the road from Franklin to Montana.

There are about 125 Indians and are riding large American horses. It is supposed to be the advande guard of Joseph's band escaping by Henry's Lake.

Chief Joseph's remarkable flight made headlines across the nation.

Instead, yet another army attacked them on the Yellowstone. And to their dismay the Nez Percés discovered that the Crow had been hired as scouts by the troops and were now aligned against them.

Their only remaining hope, Joseph and the other chiefs decided, was to leave the United States altogether. The Lakota chief Sitting Bull had fled to Canada a year earlier, after defeating General George Armstrong Custer at the Battle of the Little Bighorn. The Nez Percés headed north across the 250-mile width of Montana to join him.

Two weeks later, on September 29, as they passed the Bear Paw Mountains, Joseph's people were hungry and tired from their continuous flight. A cold wind was blowing across the treeless plains. General Howard, they knew, was more than two days' march behind them. They stopped to rest once more.

Since leaving their homes, Chief Joseph and his people had come more than fifteen hundred miles; fought in seventeen battles and skirmishes against more than two thousand soldiers and Indian scouts; and suffered hardships, disappointments, and the loss of loved ones. Now Canada—and freedom—lay only forty miles away. They planned to cross the border the next day.

Chief Joseph and his family

But at dawn on September 30, they awoke once more under attack. For nearly two weeks, Colonel Nelson A. Miles and 383 men had been hurrying from eastern Montana to intercept the Nez Percés. They rode into the camp at full gallop.

The Battle of the Bear Paw was fiercer and deadlier than all the previous fights. Fifty-three soldiers were killed or wounded. Twenty-two Nez Percés died the first day—then, as the battle became a five-day siege, even more perished. The weather turned snowy and colder. During the frigid nights, wounded children cried for their dead parents.

Hear me, my chiefs! I am tired. My heart is sick and sad. From where the sun now stands I will fight no more forever.
— *Chief Joseph*

Throughout the long flight, Joseph had been one of several chiefs making decisions. But most of the others were now dead. So Joseph was selected to ride out and negotiate with Colonel Miles. Turn over your rifles, Miles said, and in the spring you will be allowed to return home.

Some of the tribe slipped through the army lines and escaped to Canada. But Joseph was unwilling to leave the children, the old, and the wounded behind. On the afternoon of October 5, he rode out again to meet Miles and General Howard, who had finally arrived. Joseph dismounted, walked over to the officers, and surrendered his rifle.

"I am tired of fighting," he said. "Our chiefs are killed. The old men are all dead. It is cold and we have no blankets. The little children are freezing to death. My people, some of them, have run away to the hills, and have no blankets, no food. No one knows where they are—perhaps freezing to death. I want to have time to look for my children, and see how many of them I can find. Maybe I shall find them among the dead.

"Hear me, my chiefs! I am tired. My heart is sick and sad. From where the sun now stands I will fight no more forever."

The federal government never honored the promise that Colonel Miles made to Chief Joseph on the battlefield. Instead of being allowed to return home, Joseph and his people were sent to Indian Territory, in what is now Oklahoma. Unlike the dry, cool mountains of the Wallowa, it was

Chief Joseph during a visit to Washington, D.C.

humid, sweltering, and plagued by diseases such as malaria. More than a hundred of the Nez Percés died, and in despair some committed suicide in the place they called Eeikish Pah, or "the Hot Place."

In 1879 Joseph traveled to Washington, D.C., to plead for his people. There, he met with President Rutherford B. Hayes and spoke to a gathering of congressmen.

"Whenever the white man treats the Indian as they treat each other, then we shall have no more wars," he said. "There need be no trouble.

An aging Chief Joseph near his final home in exile

Treat all men alike. Give them all the same law. Give them all an even chance to live and grow. Then the Great Spirit Chief who rules above will smile upon this land, and all people may be one people."

His speech won much praise. Even many of the officers who had fought Joseph—including Miles and Howard—argued that the Nez Percés should be allowed to return to the Northwest. But the settlers there still thought Joseph and his people were dangerous, and even some Nez Percés on the Idaho reservation considered him a troublemaker. For six more years, Joseph's band remained and suffered in "the Hot Place."

At last, in 1885 Chief Joseph and his band were told they could leave Oklahoma. Half of them—mostly those who promised to convert to

Christianity—were allowed back onto the reservation in Idaho. But Joseph and 149 others were sent instead to a reservation in Washington State, among tribes unfriendly to the Nez Percés. It was far from both the Idaho reservation and the beautiful Wallowa country, where Joseph had been born and where his father and ancestors were buried.

For the rest of his life, he clung to the hope that he might someday be allowed to resettle in the homeland his people had never sold. At every chance, he used his dignity and his eloquence to argue on behalf of his band—and all Indian peoples.

Whenever the white man treats the Indian as they treat each other, then we shall have no more wars.

— *Chief Joseph*

"Let me be a free man," he said, "free to travel, free to stop, free to work, free to trade where I choose, free to follow the religion of my father, and I will obey every law or submit to the penalty."

On September 21, 1904, while sitting before his tepee fire, Chief Joseph slumped over. He had died, the reservation doctor said, of a broken heart.

Emmeline Wells

In January of 1879, a short, dainty woman named Emmeline Wells traveled east from Salt Lake City, Utah, to Washington on an important mission to speak to the president of the United States.

She was a member of the Church of Jesus Christ of Latter-day Saints—also known as the Mormons—who had moved to the West thirty years earlier in hopes of finding a place where they could practice their religion without interference.

The Mormons had been driven from New York, Ohio, Missouri, and Illinois because they believed many things that other Americans did not.

The church also owned many of Utah's businesses and had its own political party, which ran Utah Territory.

But what other people objected to most about the Mormons was their practice of plural marriage, or polygamy. Most Mormon families were not polygamous, but some Mormon men—particularly those in the church leadership—were encouraged to have more than one wife. Brigham Young, who had led the church to Utah, had twenty-seven wives and fifty-six children. Heber Kimball, Young's second in command, had forty-three wives and sixty-five children, including sixteen sons named Heber, after their father.

Now Congress and the president wanted to end Mormon control of Utah and wipe out polygamy, saying that women in plural marriages were no better off than slaves.

Brigham Young and some of his many wives

Emmeline Wells believed just the opposite and was going east to say so. The seventh wife of Daniel Wells, she was well educated, intelligent, and, despite her size, forceful and outspoken.

That every woman has an individual life, as well as every man, I am bold to affirm. — Emmeline Wells

"The world says polygamy makes women inferior to men. We think differently," she said. "Polygamy gives women more time for thought, for mental culture, more freedom of action . . . and leads women more directly to God, the fountain of all truth."

Emmeline Wells was on her way to becoming not only one of the most prominent women in Mormon history, but also a national leader in the cause of equality for *all* American women.

•◆• •◆• •◆•

As a young girl, Wells would never have predicted such a role for herself. When she graduated from New Salem Academy, in Massachusetts, at age fourteen, she converted to Mormonism and planned on becoming a

The Mormon city of Nauvoo, Illinois

school teacher. But instead, her mother set up an arranged marriage, in which Emmeline became Mrs. James Harris, even though both she and her new husband were only fifteen.

Mormonism was a new religion at the time. Emmeline and her husband immediately moved to Nauvoo, Illinois, to be closer to the church's founder, Joseph Smith. But only a few weeks later, on July 27, 1844, Smith was dead, murdered by an angry mob that disliked the Mormons. The mob threatened the other

Mormons with violence, too, unless they abandoned their homes and left Illinois. They began planning their move to Utah.

In less than a year, three other tragedies struck young Emmeline. She gave birth to a son, but the baby died. Her mother died. Then her husband deserted her. Alone, frightened, and stricken with grief, Emmeline turned to her diary.

"When will sorrow leave my bosom?" she wrote. "All my days I have experienced it. Will I forever be unhappy?"

Then, a week before her sixteenth birthday, she married Newel K. Whitney. He was thirty-three years older than she was and already had another wife. But Emmeline considered him "as good a man as ever lived" and thought that plural marriage was part of God's plan. She set out with him and her new "sister-wife" and made the long trek to Utah.

An anti-Mormon cartoon

When Whitney died unexpectedly in 1850, she was on her own once more, until she joined Daniel Wells's family as his seventh wife. Emmeline seems to be the one who proposed this marriage. In a note she called "A Letter from a True Friend," she reminded Wells of his friendship with her late husband and asked him if he had any feelings toward her.

As always, nothing came easy for Emmeline Wells. Her new husband was wealthy when they married, but soon his investments

*A*ll honor and reverence to good men; but they and their attentions are not the only source of happiness on the earth, and need not fill up every thought of women.

— Emmeline Wells

went bad. Eventually Emmeline was forced to sell the house where she and her five daughters lived. Once again, she had to struggle to survive.

*A Mormon wagon train
on its way to Utah*

"I am determined to train my girls to habits of independence," she wrote in her diary, "so that they have sufficient energy of purpose to carry out plans for their own welfare and happiness."

She applied the same rule to herself, taking a job as editor of the *Woman's Exponent,* one of the first newspapers in the West written and edited by women. In its pages, she encouraged more women to enter the workforce and argued that it was unfair for women doing the same jobs as men to be paid less. She also became a suffragist, joining the movement to win American women the right to vote.

"Millions of intelligent women are deprived of [the vote] simply because nature qualified them to become mothers and not fathers," she wrote in an editorial. "They may own property, pay taxes, assist in supporting the government, but they are denied all right to say who shall disburse those taxes, how that government shall be conducted, or who shall decide on a question of peace or war, which may involve the lives of their sons, brothers, fathers and husbands."

At the time, in early 1870, women throughout the nation were not allowed to vote. (A month earlier, Wyoming Territory had been the first to grant women political equality, but no election had yet been held there.) In Washington, D.C., a congressman suggested giving Utah women the vote,

Portrait of a polygamous family

mistakenly thinking they would use it to outlaw polygamy. The Mormons knew better, and on February 12, 1870, Utah passed its own suffrage law. Two days later, in Salt Lake City, women finally cast ballots in an American election.

•◆•

For Emmeline Wells it was an important victory, but also the start of a long struggle.

She joined the leadership of several national groups trying to extend equality to all women, not just those in Utah. In the years that followed, she would see other firsts for women and political rights, most of them in the West.

Esther Morris of South Pass City, Wyoming, became justice of the peace and America's first female office holder; Susanna Salter of Argonia, Kansas, the first woman mayor; Jeannette Rankin of Montana, the first woman elected to Congress. And back in Utah, Martha Hughes Cannon, a doctor and polygamous wife of Angus Cannon, became the first female state senator in United States history by defeating her husband at the ballot box.

Women have not asked for suffrage because of place or power, or to crowd men out of the ranks of the wage-earners or professions, but that they may be acknowledged as being equal in the work and business of the great world in which all must live and take part.

— *Emmeline Wells*

Wells's efforts on behalf of polygamy, however, were not as successful. In 1879 the president and Congress were impressed by her intelligence and eloquence, but remained committed to stopping plural marriage and weakening the Mormon church's power in Utah. Over the following years, federal laws were passed that made polygamy illegal, threw many Mormon men into jail, and threatened the religion's entire existence.

Finally, in 1890, the Mormon church disbanded its political party, sold most of its businesses, and gave up the practice of polygamy. In return, Utah was allowed to switch from a territory to a state.

Wells, meanwhile, kept writing for the *Woman's Exponent*. She became president of the Mormon church's important Relief Society and was the first woman to receive an honorary doctorate from Brigham Young University. She was a featured speaker at national and international women's conferences. And on five more occasions, she met with United States presidents to talk about women's issues and the Mormon religion.

Even in old age,
Emmeline Wells fought
for the rights of women.

"I believe in women, especially thinking women," she said. "I desire to do all in my power to help elevate the condition of my people, especially women."

Emmeline Wells was definitely a thinking woman. And she accomplished a lot—for her people and for other women. On April 25, 1921, one year after the U.S. Constitution was amended to grant all women the right to vote, she died at age ninety-three.

I believe in women, especially thinking women.

— *Emmeline Wells*

Pap Singleton

In the summer of 1879, thousands of African Americans left their homes in the South and began moving west. Some went by riverboat up the Mississippi and Missouri Rivers. A few went by train. But many of them were too poor to buy tickets and *walked* more than five hundred miles from Mississippi, Louisiana, Kentucky, and Tennessee, all the way to the prairies of Kansas, for the chance of a better life.

They called themselves Exodusters, after the old story in the Bible's book of Exodus about the migration of the Hebrews out of Egypt. Just as the Hebrews had Moses to guide them to their Promised Land, the Exodusters were following a remarkable leader to Kansas.

His name was Benjamin "Pap" Singleton. And his lifelong dream was of freedom — not just for himself, but for all African Americans.

•◆• •◆• •◆•

Pap Singleton was born into slavery in Nashville, Tennessee, in 1809. As a young man, he was sold more than twelve times. But Singleton did not consider himself someone else's property. Three times he ran away, only to be captured and returned to his owner. Finally, he escaped to

Slaves coming in from the cotton fields on a southern plantation

Canada by traveling what was called the Underground Railroad—the network of farms and homes of people who sheltered runaway slaves on their way to safety.

After the Civil War made slavery illegal, Singleton returned to

Conditions might be better a hundred years from now when all the present generation's dead and gone but not afore, sir, not afore, and what's going to be a hundred years from now ain't much account to us in this present of the Lord.
— Pap Singleton

Tennessee. But he soon learned that conditions for black people in the South were still very bad. Most newly freed slaves did not have enough

Picking cotton . . .

*and planting
sweet potatoes*

money to buy their own farms and were forced into sharecropping, or renting land from their former masters, who often still considered them to be inferior people. Under those conditions, it was almost impossible for sharecroppers to save enough money to get ahead. "I works hard and raises big crops," a sharecropper named John Solomon Lewis told his landlord, "and you sells it and keeps the money and brings me more and more in debt."

At the rate things were going, Singleton said, conditions would not improve for his people for a hundred more years. "The whites has the lands," he said, "an' the blacks has nothin' but their freedom, an' it's jest like a dream to them."

Like other African-American leaders of the time, Singleton believed that the former slaves needed to own their land, not rent it, if their lives

were going to improve. Some favored starting a colony in the African republic of Liberia. Others wanted to move to Canada.

Singleton had a different idea. He believed that true freedom could be found in the West. In the South, all the farmland was already privately owned and was too expensive for former slaves to buy. But in the West, the government was still offering 160-acre homesteads to anyone who paid a ten-dollar fee and then worked the land for five years.

In 1873 he took a scouting trip to Kansas. He returned to Tennessee to persuade three hundred people to move to a place called the Singleton Colony, in the southeastern corner of the state. Then he started plans to recruit even more African Americans to move to Kansas.

He printed up thousands of leaflets about the opportunities for former slaves to own farms in the West. "Come and join us in the promised land," one advertisement read. He gave them to preachers in black churches and to African-American workers on railroads and steamboats, asking them all to spread the word. Songs were written, urging share-croppers to abandon their rented farms in the South for a new chance in Kansas. "Marching along, yes we are marching along," one song said, adding that Singleton "will go on before us and lead us through."

Ho for Kansas!

Brethren, Friends, & Fellow Citizens:
I feel thankful to inform you that the
REAL ESTATE
AND
Homestead Association,
Will Leave Here the
15th of April, 1878,
In pursuit of Homes in the Southwestern Lands of America, at Transportation Rates, cheaper than ever was known before.
For full information inquire of
Benj. Singleton, better known as old Pap,
NO. 5 NORTH FRONT STREET.
Beware of Speculators and Adventurers, as it is a dangerous thing to fall in their hands.
Nashville, Tenn., March 18, 1878.

Pap Singleton flooded the South with fliers like this one.

*S*ays the captain, "Where's you going?"
Says I, "Kansas."
— *John Solomon Lewis*

Soon small numbers of African Americans were scattered throughout Kansas, and their hopeful letters home were being read aloud in black churches.

Then, in the spring of 1879, a rumor started circulating in the South. It said that the government had set aside *all* of Kansas for former slaves and would provide every black family that could get there with free land and

Waiting for a boat headed for the West

five hundred dollars. The rumor wasn't true, but it set off the biggest migration of Exodusters yet. Nearly twenty thousand African Americans that year risked everything they had, migrating to a land they had never seen.

To those who marveled at why so many sharecroppers would take the long journey, Pap Singleton had a simple explanation. "It is because they are poor that they want to get away," he said. "If they had plenty, they wouldn't want to come. It's to better their condition that they are thinking of. That's what white men go to new countries for, isn't it?" Singleton kept on recruiting.

Some of the African Americans lived in Kansas's bigger cities, but

It is because they are poor that they want to get away. If they had plenty they wouldn't want to come. It's to better their condition that they are thinking of. That's what white men go to new countries for, isn't it?

— *Pap Singleton*

98

Nicodemus, Kansas

most of them were on farms and in small communities such as Juniper Town, Dunlap, and Rattlebone Hollow. Nicodemus, in western Kansas, was the largest settlement of Exodusters, home to seven hundred settlers from Kentucky.

An Exoduster's new home in Kansas

An Exoduster school

Out on the prairies, the Exodusters faced the same hardships that challenged all pioneers. There were dry times when crops failed and wet times when floods ruined everything. There were hard times when the prices that farmers were paid for cattle and corn collapsed below what it cost to raise them. And while some white settlers welcomed their black neighbors, others shunned them or even tried to drive them away.

But just like all the pioneers who came west, the Exodusters responded in many different ways. Some gave up and returned to the South, defeated by the harsh climate of the plains. Some picked up and tried again even farther west. And many of them stuck it out, forging out new lives for themselves and their families in the place Pap Singleton had called the Promised Land.

Some moved on, but many stuck it out in Kansas.

Years later, Pap Singleton was bitterly disappointed that more African Americans had not answered his call to join him in the West. In fact he

decided that the best thing for blacks in the United States might be to get out altogether and start colonies in Africa. But even fewer people followed that advice.

He was eighty-three and poor when he died in 1892 at Topeka, Kansas. But the dream he had once held for so many African Americans had at least been found by some.

I asked my wife did she know the ground she stands on. She said, "No."
I said it is free ground and she cried for joy.

— *John Solomon Lewis*

John Solomon Lewis was one of them. When he crossed into Kansas, he remembered, "I looked on the ground and I says this is free ground.

"Then I looked on the heavens and I says them is free and beautiful heavens. Then I looked within my heart and I says to myself I wonder why I was never free before? I asked my wife did she know the ground she stands on. She said, 'No.' I said it is free ground and she cried for joy."

Free ground: one of the oldest and most enduring dreams of the West. And Pap Singleton, the "father of the Exodus," had worked to make that dream a reality.

Pap Singleton
saw the West as the
"Promised Land."

Buffalo Bird Woman and Wolf Chief

In 1885 the Hidatsa Indians of North Dakota were living together on a hill overlooking the Missouri River in a village they called Like-a-Fish-hook. Their homes were earth lodges, large round dwellings made of tree trunks and twigs covered with dirt and grass. The land they occupied and farmed was owned by the entire tribe. Most Hidatsas still followed tribal customs and traditions that dated back to before the arrival of white men, 150 years earlier.

But now the United States government wanted it all to change.

People who called themselves "Friends of the Indians" believed that Native Americans would be better off giving up their old way of life and becoming more like white Americans—speaking English, becoming

Christians, and owning small plots of land individually rather than communally, as a group. No one asked the Indians if that was what *they* wanted.

The Hidatsas were ordered to abandon Like-a-Fishhook village and move out to small family farms separated from one another. As they left, the government had their old earth lodges destroyed, to prevent them from coming back.

The earth lodge village of the Hidatsas in 1870

Among the last to leave were the families of Buffalo Bird Woman and her brother Wolf Chief. The new place they settled was a hill that had been chosen by Wolf Chief in a dream vision that had come to him after fasting. They called it Awatahesh, "hill by itself." White people translated it as Independence.

Independence turned out to be a good name for their new home, because both Buffalo Bird Woman and Wolf Chief proved themselves to be independent people. Like Native Americans throughout the West in those times, they faced many challenges and dramatic changes. But instead of responding in exactly the way they were told to, both of them made their own choices.

Buffalo Bird Woman would choose to hold on to the old ways as much as possible.

Wolf Chief would choose to "walk the white man's road" but in his own way.

•◆• •◆• •◆•

Forty years earlier, they had been born into a much different world.

In the 1830s, their grandfather, a greatly respected man among the tribe, was in charge of taking care of an ancient and sacred "medicine bundle," which the Hidatsas believed brought them help from spirits in war, in hunting, and in bringing rain for their crops. The bundle included two human skulls wrapped in a blanket and had been passed along from one generation to another for centuries.

"How do we know there are spirits, Grandfather?" young Buffalo Bird Woman had asked.

"*Little granddaughter," my grandfather said, "this earth is alive and has a soul or spirit, just as you have a spirit. Other things also have spirits, the sun, clouds, trees, beasts, birds. These spirits are our gods. We pray to them and offer them food, that they may help us when we have need.*" — Buffalo Bird Woman

"They appear to us in our dreams," he answered. "That is why the medicine man fasts and cuts his flesh with knives. If he fasts long, he will fall in a vision. In this vision, the spirits will come and talk with him."

Young Hidatsas were taught that everything had a spirit. "We thought that the corn plants had souls, as children have souls," Buffalo Bird Woman remembered. "We thought that our growing corn liked to hear us sing, just as children like to hear their mother sing to them."

She learned to weave baskets and mats, make pots from clay, and decorate buffalo robes with paint and porcupine quills. Most crafts were considered sacred, and a young girl had to purchase the rights to learn them from older women. As a gift, her mother taught her the ceremonies

Buffalo Bird Woman weaving a mat out of rushes

for making an earth lodge—a special talent that earned Buffalo Bird Woman many robes from other families.

According to Hidatsa customs, women owned what they made—the crops they grew, the clothes they sewed, the earth lodges they built. And when a couple married, the man moved into his wife's home. So it was important for young girls to acquire many skills.

We thought an earth lodge was alive and had a spirit like a human body, and that its front was like a face, with the door for mouth. — Buffalo Bird Woman

"If a girl was a worker and tanned hundreds of hides, her aunt might give her an honor mark," Buffalo Bird Woman said. "My aunt Sage gave me a woman's belt. It was broad as my three fingers and covered with blue beads. Only a very industrious girl was given such a belt. She could not buy or make one. I was as proud of mine as a war leader of his first scalp."

But Hidatsa girls also had time for fun. Buffalo Bird Woman had dolls made of deerskin and antelope hair. In winter, she raced down hills on

Wolf Chief as a young man, 1879

sleds made from curved buffalo ribs. And she played games. In one, girls with hooked sticks tried to knock a leather ball past another team's goals. In another, they kicked a large, soft ball with their toes and knees, seeing who could keep it from touching the ground for the longest time.

Boys had special games, too. One of Wolf Chief's favorites was played in the summer. The boys would divide into teams and have pretend battles, using long, flexible willow sticks to hurl mud balls, sometimes as far as a hundred yards. "Before the mud balls reached us, we could hear them *hw-i-ɔ-ɔ* like a whistle . . . as they flew through the air," he remembered. "The lump of mud hit the boy on the face or body and fell with a *ɔpat* and made the boy cry very often."

At age four, Wolf Chief got his first bow and arrows and learned to use them by shooting at mice in his family's earth lodge. As he grew older, his father taught him to hunt. Out hunting one winter, the bright sun reflecting on the snow nearly made him blind; a blizzard began, and Wolf Chief nearly froze to death, finally seeking shelter by climbing into a porcupine's den.

White people seem to think that Indian children never have any play and never laugh. Such ideas seem very funny to me. How can any child grow up without play? We Indian children also had games. I think they were better than white children's games.

— *Buffalo Bird Woman*

By the time he was sixteen, he was hunting buffalo on horseback, learning to ride to within a few feet of a stampeding buffalo and shoot with enough strength to bury his arrow up to its end feathers in the animal's side. A respected hunter, he was taught, should share what he killed with other people. "To give it away was the right thing to do, and it was like winning an honor mark," he said. "If a man wanted to be good, he must not be selfish."

At sixteen, Wolf Chief went on his first war party, against the Hidatsas' enemies the Lakota, or Sioux. His job was to fetch water and firewood on the trail, while older, more experienced warriors did the fighting.

Warfare was more than battling for land, stealing valuable horses, or taking captives from other tribes. It was also seen as a way for a man to show bravery, leadership, and spiritual powers. But it was always dangerous. Wolf Chief joined a group called the Stone Hammer Society, a special group of boys with its own ceremonies and rituals. (Buffalo Bird Woman belonged to the Skunk Society, a group of girls who performed dances to celebrate victories over enemies.) Of the forty boys who joined the Stone Hammers with Wolf Chief, eight were killed in war before they reached age thirty.

When a man put his sacred objects outside his lodge, it meant "I want all the gods to know that I am going on a war party, so that they will give me protection." It was also a notice to the people that he was forming a war party and was an invitation to the young men of the village to join it. — Wolf Chief

Before he could enter his first battle, Wolf Chief had to gain the protection of spirits. Every night for four months, he went off by himself to fast and pray. Finally, he had a dream that told him he would become a respected warrior and lead successful war parties.

Over the next years, he proved that his vision had been right. He earned many honor marks — feathers, horsehair, and wood carvings, which he attached to his clothes — and which symbolized his brave deeds.

As they became adults, Wolf Chief and Buffalo Bird Woman continued leading lives that would have been familiar to their grandfather the medicine man. Wolf Chief hunted buffalo, went on war parties against the Lakota and

Three Mandans, allies of the Hidatsas, in ceremonial clothes

other enemy tribes, and practiced the Hidatsas' traditional religion. Buffalo Bird Woman took care of her earth lodge, planted her gardens, and sang to her corn crops. In 1868 she married a warrior named Son of Star, after his family gave hers four prize horses. The next year, while the tribe was following a buffalo herd near the Yellowstone River, she gave birth to her first and only child.

Before the birth, her mother, Strikes Many Women, performed a special ceremony believed to help women when they had babies. Her father, Small Ankle, prayed for assistance from the sacred medicine bundle that had belonged to Buffalo Bird Woman's grandfather. The baby—a boy they named Goodbird—was born on a cold night, in a tent on a sandbar in the river.

Son of Star and Buffalo Bird Woman with their son, Goodbird

Soon, however, the lives of all the Hidatsas would dramatically change. And the paths of Buffalo Bird Woman and her brother Wolf Chief would take different directions.

When they were forced to leave Like-a-Fishhook village in 1885, the Hidatsas were told to live in square log cabins instead of their traditional earth lodges. Buffalo Bird Woman did not like this change. All the special skills and ceremonies she had learned in making earth lodges were suddenly considered useless. As a connection to their past, her husband, Son of Star, placed a buffalo skull over the door of their new cabin, and their woodstove was set in the center of the house, where an earth lodge fire would have been.

But for her, it was not the same. Other changes troubled her, too.

The buffalo were gone now, slaughtered for their hides by white hunters who swarmed to the northern Great Plains riding the new railroads. The herds had once numbered in the millions, and the Hidatsas, like many other tribes, had depended on them for food, clothing, utensils, and sacred ceremonies. Amazingly, within Buffalo Bird Woman's lifetime, the buffalo had disappeared. "When the buffalo went away, the hearts of my people fell to the ground, and they could not lift them up again," another Indian woman remembered. "There was little singing anywhere."

Unlike some other tribes, which depended entirely on the buffalo for food, the Hidatsas had always been farmers as well as hunters. But now the government agent on their reservation told them to plant different crops—flax and wheat and potatoes.

"These potatoes we Indians did not like at first, because they smelled strong," Buffalo Bird Woman said. "We... often left them in the ground, not bothering even to dig them."

Instead, she kept planting her traditional crops of beans, squash, and corn. And she used her traditional hoe, instead of new machines, and her traditional ceremonies in her garden. One year, she entered her corn in a contest run by the agent. It won first prize—and it was grown, she said, "exactly as in old times."

Goodbird's wife, Sioux Woman, hoeing squash with a traditional bone hoe

In the effort to make Native Americans more like white people, Indian children were separated from their parents and sent to schools where they were forbidden to speak their native language, wear traditional clothing, or grow their hair long, as had been their custom. The government encouraged missionaries to go to reservations and convert the Indians to the Christian religion. Medicine bundles, which connected Indians to the spirit world, were

A mission school at Like-a-Fishhook village. Indian traditions, including wearing the hair long, were forbidden at reservation schools.

to be burned. Ancient ceremonies, such as dances and songs, were not permitted.

Like many other Indians, Buffalo Bird Woman resisted. She held on to her customs, her language, and her beliefs. "I [do not] like white men's laws," she said. "I do not understand them nor know how to make them rule my life."

But Wolf Chief, unlike his sister, came to believe that learning the white man's ways would be good for him—and for his people. At the age of thirty, he decided to learn arithmetic and English.

The buffaloes and black-tail deer are gone, and our Indian ways are almost gone.... We no longer live in an earth lodge, but in a house with chimneys; and my son's wife cooks by a stove. But for me, I cannot forget the old ways.

— Buffalo Bird Woman

On his first day at school, he showed up dressed in the way he had always dressed for special occasions. "I painted my face red, long hair braided, wore . . . a bead necklace . . . & round pearl shells on either breast," he said.

110

"I wore . . . a blanket and shirt of white sheeting, leggings of blanket cloth and moccasins."

Wolf Chief was eager to learn and became a dedicated student. Soon he was good at numbers and could speak and write English. He was proud of his achievement.

"When Indians come to a white man's store for bacon and think [he] cannot understand them, they make signs like a flat curled-up nose for pig & go unh-unh—grunting," he boasted. "But when I go to a store, I say 'bacon' and get it right away."

He opened his own store on the reservation so his people would not have to travel so far for goods and depend on white men who did not speak their language. When his store began doing well, the reservation agent's brother decided to get into the business. Wolf Chief was told to close his store.

Instead, he used his new skills and wrote to the head of Indian Affairs in Washington, D.C. A government inspector was sent to the reservation to look into the matter. The other store was shut down. Wolf Chief's store stayed open.

Wolf Chief kept on writing letters to Washington. He wrote more than a hundred before he was through. He complained of agents cheating the Hidatsas, asked for food when his people were hungry, and urged that broken-down reservation buildings be fixed. Some of his letters were sent to the president himself. In them, he often ended with the words, "Your friend, Mr. Wolf C. Chief."

He became a judge on the reservation and persuaded some of his neighbors to take up stock ranching, to raise their own

Wolf Chief at his store

Wolf Chief with his wife,
Female Coyote, and son,
Frank Wolf Chief

cattle to replace the missing buffalo. Finally, Wolf Chief converted to Christianity. He even donated ten acres of his own land so a chapel could be built near his cabin.

"I am going to see if God will not help me," he said. "If God will help me so that I have plenty, and if God gives me a long life, I am sure his way will be best."

My people often talk against me & laugh & say, "That man wants to be a white man."...[But] I want to be strong and go forward. — Wolf Chief

"My people often talk against me & laugh & say, 'That man wants to be a white man.' ...[But] I want to be strong and go forward." "I have changed my ways and become Christian, but...one way I have not changed. When poor people and hungry people come for food, I cannot refuse them. I am sure that Jesus fed people when He was on earth."

By the early 1900s, both Buffalo Bird Woman and Wolf Chief were growing old. And both remained true to the different paths they had chosen.

Buffalo Bird Woman continued to resist any changes in the way she lived. She spoke only the Hidatsa language and practiced her traditional religion. When her husband, Son of Star, died in 1906, she mourned his passing in the old Hidatsa way—she cut her hair short and wore it loose, and she sliced off the tip of a little finger.

"Often in summer I rise at daybreak and steal out to the cornfields," she said. "And as I hoe the corn, I sing to it, as we did when I was young. No one cares for our corn songs now."

At sunset, she would sit on a hill, looking at the big Missouri River, one of the few things that hadn't changed during her lifetime.

"In the shadows I seem again to see our Indian village, with smoke curling upward from the earth lodges; and in the river's roar I hear the yells of the warriors, the laughter of little children as of old.

"It is but an old woman's dream. Again I see but shadows and hear only the roar of the river; and tears come into my eyes. Our Indian life, I know, is gone forever."

She never abandoned the beliefs her grandfather had taught her.

Buffalo Bird Woman, with her son and granddaughter. To mourn her husband's death, she sliced off the tip of her little finger.

Before she died, in the 1920s, she agreed to tell her life story and explain her people's traditions to a writer. That way, she decided, she could be sure they would never be forgotten.

Wolf Chief continued on the "white man's road" the rest of his life. He did keep one connection to the old ways, though—his grandfather's sacred medicine bundle, which he kept in a small earth lodge near his cabin. Missionaries and reservation agents urged him to destroy it. Out of respect for his ancestors, Wolf Chief refused.

But he grew worried about it. If he kept the bundle, he might anger his new Christian God. But by no longer believing in the spirits of his grandfather, he might also be angering *them*. None of the other Hidatsas, however, were willing to keep the medicine bundle, with the special ceremonies and powers it was supposed to possess. Finally, to keep it from being either neglected or destroyed, he sold it to a museum in New York and felt relieved of his burden.

Wolf Chief demonstrates a prayer for rain in an earth lodge.

Like Buffalo Bird Woman, Wolf Chief also thought a lot about his life when he looked at the Missouri River from the hill called Independence.

He had chosen that place many years earlier, guided by his dream vision. But his view was different from his sister's.

"All that I saw in that dream has come true," he said before he died, in 1934. "I have prospered here and am a hale old man, though my former wife died here and my children, but then they never had this dream. Perhaps it was God who gave me that dream. I do not know. I only know that all that I saw in that dream has come true."

The story of Buffalo Bird Woman and Wolf Chief, and the two roads they followed, would not be complete without telling what happened to the sacred medicine bundle that had belonged to their grandfather.

The bundle represented the old ways that the sister had clung to and the brother rejected. But it was Wolf Chief who had kept it from being destroyed when no one else would take care of it.

The sacred medicine bundle was finally returned to the Hidatsas.

Shortly before his death, Wolf Chief wrote his last letter to Washington. In it he described the terrible dry weather that had gripped the Great Plains for several years. It was killing the crops and ruining many farmers — Indians and whites alike. The once-abundant plains, it was said, had become a giant Dust Bowl.

In 1938 the Hidatsas asked the New York museum to return the sacred bundle to them. This was the beginning of a nationwide movement for Indian tribes to reclaim items that held special religious meaning to them. The return of the medicine bundle to Independence was one of the first cases in which this happened.

And the summer it was brought back to its old home, rain fell once again on the plains.

Principal Sources

Sweet Medicine

Grinnell, George Bird. The Cheyenne Indians. New Haven: Yale University Press, 1923; Lincoln: University of Nebraska Press, 1972.

Stands in Timber, John, and Margot Liberty. *Cheyenne Memories*. New Haven: Yale University Press, 1967.

Cabeza de Vaca

Covey, Cyclone, translator and editor. *Cabeza de Vaca's Adventures in the Unknown Interior of America*. Albuquerque: University of New Mexico Press, 1961.

Kit Carson

Carter, Harvey Lewis. *Dear Old Kit: The Historical Christopher Carson*. Norman, Okla.: University of Oklahoma Press, 1968.

Narcissa Whitman

Jeffrey, Julie Roy. *Converting the West: A Biography of Narcissa Whitman*. Norman, Okla.: University of Oklahoma Press, 1991.

Mariano Guadalupe Vallejo

McKittrick, Myrtle M. *Vallejo, Son of California*. N.p.: Binfords and Mort, 1944.

"Mariano Guadalupe Vallejo and Sonoma." *California Historical Society Quarterly*, vol. 16, no. 2 (1937).

William Swain

Holliday, J. S. *The World Rushed In: An Eyewitness Account of a Nation Heading West*. New York: Simon and Schuster, 1981.

"John Chinaman" Builds a Railroad

Chen, Jack. *The Chinese of America.* New York: Harper & Row, 1980.

Williams, John Hoyt. *A Great and Shining Road.* New York: Times Books, 1988.

Teddy Blue Abbott

Abbott, E. C., and Helena Huntington Smith. *We Pointed Them North: Recollections of a Cowpuncher.* Norman, Okla.: University of Oklahoma Press, 1939.

Uriah and Mattie Oblinger

Letters of the Oblinger family, Nebraska State Historical Society.

Chief Joseph

Josephy, Alvin M., Jr. *The Nez Perce Indians and the Opening of the Northwest.* Lincoln: University of Nebraska Press, 1965.

Lavender, David. *Let Me Be Free: The Nez Perce Tragedy.* New York: Harper Collins, 1992.

Emmeline Wells

Madsen, Carol Cornwall. "Emmeline Wells: Am I Not a Woman and a Sister?" *Brigham Young University Studies,* vol. 22, no. 2 (1982).

Pap Singleton

Painter, Nell Irvine. *Exodusters: Black Migration to Kansas After Reconstruction.* New York: Norton, 1976.

Buffalo Bird Woman and Wolf Chief

Gilman, Carolyn, and Mary Jane Schneider. *The Way to Independence: Memories of a Hidatsa Indian Family, 1840–1920.* St. Paul: Minnesota Historical Society Press, 1987.

Waheenee, as told to Gilbert L. Wilson. *Waheenee: An Indian Girl's Story.* Lincoln: University of Nebraska Press, 1981.

Index

Photography Credits